Dedicated to the little food explorers of this world – may these early lessons bring you messy faces, full tummies and happy hearts.

Real Food
for **Babies**
& **Toddlers**

✳

Baby-led weaning and beyond,
with over **80 wholefood** recipes
the whole family will love

VANESSA CLARKSON

MURDOCH BOOKS
SYDNEY · LONDON

Contents

Learning to Love Real Food

Question: Are we born liking some foods and disliking others, or do we learn what appeals to us and what doesn't?

If we truly aspire to fostering a love of real food in our children, understanding how much of this is in our hands – nurture – versus how much is out of our hands – nature – can have a huge impact on our resolve. And when I say resolve, what I mean is the doggedness that you are going to need in order to persevere with offering your child the broccoli or the hummus or the [*insert here whatever food you want your child to love*] when they are adamant that they are *not* going to eat what you have lovingly prepared for them. Not for all the tea in China or all the toys in the toyshop, as it were.

Well, quite simply, I can answer this question by telling you that children eat what they like and like what they know. In other words, we learn. We learn to like broccoli, just as we learn to ride a bike, and just like riding a bike it takes practice, practice and more practice.

Sure, some foods are naturally easier for us to like, and there are reasons for that, which I will talk about shortly. But just know that it's all up for grabs. It may not necessarily be easy, but it is entirely possible to teach our children to love real food. And food school starts sooner than you think.

Food school

You won't recall the first time you ever tasted an apple – and not simply because you were too young to remember, but also because you weren't even born when it happened. Lessons begin when we're but a bundle of cells. From as early as 8 weeks after conception, our tastebuds start to appear. By halfway through pregnancy, we pass at least some of our days mastering the art of sucking and swallowing. With plenty of time to practise, fast-forward to a month or so before we're born and we have actually become quite good at this new skill, enjoying as much as a litre (35 fl oz) of amniotic fluid each day.

Our indisputable first food, amniotic fluid is ever changing in flavour depending on what a mother eats. We know this because scientists have been able to take samples and can tell us correctly whether a mother has recently eaten garlic or spices, inhaled tobacco and so on. And so before we've even been born, before we've taken our first breath, we've already unknowingly learned quite a lot about the world of food we are about to enter.

Food school continues as a baby is fed breast milk. With breast milk, whatever a mother enjoys for breakfast, her baby will sample for lunch. As with amniotic fluid, the flavour of breast milk varies. From an evolutionary perspective, this transfer of flavours offers a survival advantage – teaching our young what is OK and safe to consume, preparing them for a time when they can and are expected to feed themselves. For most babies, the transition to 'solid' food – generally referred to as 'weaning' or 'complementary feeding' – begins around the 6-month mark. Over time, babies gradually increase their consumption of solids and reduce their reliance on breast milk (or infant formula), to meet their nutritional requirements.

Life in a baby bubble

Babies and young children live in a completely different sensory world from older children and adults. If we look at sweetness, for example, all babies are born liking it, and their preference is especially high during growth spurts. Indeed, it's probably truer

... before we've even taken our first breath, we've already unknowingly learned quite a lot about the world of food that we are about to enter.

to say that little ones do not just like sweetness, they adore it. To put this in perspective, one of the largest studies to look at this (involving more than 900 participants) found that, given the choice, children preferred a sugar concentration equivalent to 11 teaspoons or about 45 g (1½ oz) of sugar in a 200 ml (7 fl oz) glass of water. That is more than twice the amount found in popular brands of cola! Not until later in adolescence does this liking for sweetness start to dip to the sort of level we're familiar with as adults.

When it comes to saltiness, on the other hand, newborns are quite indifferent to it. From somewhere between 2 and 6 months of age, they can spot salty flavours, and this develops into a stronger preference between 3 and 11 years of age – again, at a more heightened level than we would be used to experiencing as adults.

Conversely, little ones generally don't show an innate liking for bitter or sour flavours. This makes sense when you consider that in nature you would more likely associate bitter flavours with toxic or poisonous substances, whereas sweet and salty would indicate nutritious, energy-, vitamin- and mineral-rich foods.

Nature versus nurture

These in-built preferences for sweet and salty, and the rejection of bitter flavours, offer what can be seen as a loose framework within which a child's food choices are made. This means that little ones will find liking sweet and salty food easier than liking bitter. Still, that doesn't make it true to say that we're genetically programmed to prefer a narrow range of foods – quite the opposite, in fact. Humans are omnivores, and our survival over the millennia has hinged on our ability to thrive on a wide range of foods. And so our food likes and dislikes are shaped principally by our experiences. In other words, we learn through exposure.

Researchers in this area believe that repeated exposure to certain foods, leading to their acceptance, works in a number of ways. Predominantly it is about familiarisation and a primal sense of safety. We come to trust the food – we know what it tastes and smells like; what it feels like in our mouths and stomachs; and, most importantly when it comes to a vulnerable baby, that it will not make us ill, or perhaps worse.

What's more, our food preferences are much more flexible the younger we are. Babies are generally quite accepting of new foods. Even if you find that they comically screw up their face at something new, more often than not, they're very happy to trust you and explore what you have offered them.

Unfortunately, just as you're getting to grips with this eating lark, from around your child's first birthday, the amount of food deliberately thrown on the floor, at the wall, at you or fed to the dog often starts to increase. Fast-forward to their third birthday, and you've come to realise that, while you were catching up on the sleep that you didn't get in their first year, someone swapped your cute and squidgy little baby for a pint-sized dictator, capable of forming and acting upon their own opinions. And often that opinion is no. No, I don't want this food any more. I know I liked it yesterday and for the past three years of my life on this planet, but no. Take it away.

I believe that it's in our response to these inevitable showdowns and how we make the most of those very early days, when babies are open and willing to be taught, that we can lay the foundations of eating well. And this is the reason for this book. It's not just our likes and dislikes that are established early on, but also our long-term health.

Little people, big decisions

Some animals enter this world and pretty much hit the ground running. Foals, for example, are able to stand up and walk around within their first hour. Quite a feat, really, when you compare them with us and reflect on how utterly dependent and vulnerable we are on the day of our birth, and indeed for a long time after.

Consider just one example: our brains. At birth they are only 30 per cent of their adult size. One obvious reason for this (to which many mothers can attest) is that women would really struggle to get a bigger-headed baby out. Beyond that, women would also be pregnant for a lot longer. Instead, nature compromises and makes up for this by completing a truly humungous brain growth spurt, so that by our second birthday our brain has burgeoned to 80 per cent of its adult weight; by our sixth birthday it is at 95 per cent.

Now, we're going to need an awful lot in the way of nutrients from our food to support that sort of growth, and many of those nutrients are what we call essential. In other words, we have to get them from our diet – there is no other option. We can't make them or magic them out of thin air. If there's a gap, the body has to make do, and the development that was supposed to happen simply can't occur to its full potential.

This matters even more because, broadly speaking, once an organ is made, the job is pretty much done. Sure, you're going to spend a lot of your life tending to that organ, nurturing and repairing it, but its foundations are set in the very early days, months and years. And, like the foundations of a house, these support us for the rest of our lives. Do a shoddy job on one of them, and cracks will appear sooner or later.

To show what a difference the availability of nutrients can make, let's consider breastfeeding for a moment. Breast milk has been designed by nature to match precisely a baby's nutritional requirements, so it should come as no surprise that breastfed babies score higher on tests of cognitive development than those who are formula-fed. All else being equal, their brains have been given exactly the right nutrition to support optimal growth.

In the largest randomised controlled trial done in this area, involving nearly 14,000 babies, the Promotion of Breastfeeding Intervention Trial found that, even after accounting for a range of other influential factors such as a mother's level of education and socioeconomic status, prolonged, exclusive breastfeeding can result in an average IQ score nearly 6 points higher by the age of 6.

Babies are generally quite accepting of new foods. Even if you find that they comically screw up their face at something new, more often than not, they're very happy to trust you and explore what you have offered them.

Similar consequences have been seen when it comes to food: scientists have investigated how different diets can impact brain development. The UK-based Avon Longitudinal Study of Parents and Children (ALSPAC) involved about 14,000 babies (now adults) born between April 1991 and December 1992. Researchers looked at a subset of more than 7000 ALSPAC participants and what they typically ate when they were 6 months, 15 months and 24 months old, then tracked them over time to take measurements of their IQ at both 8 and 15 years of age.

The researchers found a link between IQ in adolescence (a predictor of adult IQ) and a healthier diet in the first two years of life. The healthier diet included more wholefoods such as raw fruit and vegetables, herbs, legumes, cheese and fish. Conversely, those who ate less wholesome foods as babies – such as potato chips (crisps), biscuits (cookies), confectionery (candy), chocolate and sugary drinks – had a lower IQ as teenagers. This was true even after researchers took into account other factors such as socioeconomic status that could have driven a difference.

I don't want to sound preachy or cause panic by sharing this. You don't need me adding to the big pile of pressure you already feel as a parent. My aim is simply to show that what we feed our babies and children truly does matter, and investing whatever time and energy you can to this really will pay off. Not just in terms of establishing broad and healthy taste preferences – you could argue that someone who has a poor diet when they're little can make up for it when they're old enough to know better – but also because it will lay the nourishing foundations that will give them a good shot at enjoying a long and healthy life. And that's what this is all about, right?

Inner health

It's also worth discussing our microscopic tenants: the 100 trillion bacterial cells that live within our bodies. More commonly referred to collectively as our microbiota, or 'little life', they're as fundamental to our good health and survival as we are to theirs. As the food we eat feeds them as well as us, it's worth mentioning these microscopic

tenants briefly. Collectively, our microbiota may weigh as much as 2 kg (4½ lb). Nearly all of these bacteria hang out in our gut, from where they perform a vast array of helpful tasks. The microbiota is exceptionally important for babies. It supports the development of their immature immune system and helps with the digestion and absorption of food, including producing nutrients that play a major role in promoting normal growth – for instance, B vitamins, some amino acids and essential fats, as well as vitamin K (which is needed for blood clotting).

Our microbiota endures a continuous battle for survival, with the health-promoting good guys on one side and the harmful bad guys on the other. Scientists are just at the frontier of deciphering which factors contribute to the upsetting and restoring of this balance, as well as understanding how an imbalance, particularly when we're very young, can be linked to an expanding list of health effects, both in the short and long term. These health effects include atopic diseases such as asthma, allergies and eczema; autoimmune diseases such as type 1 diabetes and coeliac disease; and inflammatory bowel diseases.

Four main factors in our early years contribute to the establishment of a healthy microbiota: the pioneer bunch of heirloom bacteria we are given while still in the womb; the hitchhikers that join us on our way out into the world, such as those present in the birth canal; breast milk topping us up with more than 700 species of bacteria; and, last but by no means least, the foods onto which we are weaned, which provide their own bacteria as well as nourishment to the little folk already present in our gut. And those first 18 months of foods are crucial because our microbiota has already established itself and stabilised by our second birthday.

Researchers have repeatedly found that people who consume plant-based diets typically have a healthier microbial population in their gut. This is not rocket science, really, because plant-based foods are high in fibre. 'Fibre', of course, is the collective term for a big group of carbohydrates that humans can't digest, but the good bacteria can – and do so through a process called 'fermentation'. In providing the good guys with plenty of the food that they like, you are effectively giving them the supplies they need to be fighting fit and keeping the bad guys in check, as well as to produce all those valuable nutrients mentioned earlier.

The First 1000 Days

This incredibly influential window of opportunity for investing in the nourishing foundations that support lifelong optimal health is known as the 'First 1000 Days'. This is the time when our bodies grow at a pace never to be repeated at any other time in our lives; when we form our opinions on those foods we like and those we do not, and when our microbiota settles in, ready to join us for this ride.

In this book I hope to support parents who want to successfully negotiate and make the most of this time, by providing the foundations of a wholesome diet, powered mostly by plants and offered in a manner that supports their baby's development in every way possible. A different way: one that means not starting off on the miserable (and never-ending for some) path of making separate meals for little ones; one that doesn't involve meal plans or instructions on introducing your carrots before your cucumbers. Just honest, commonsense advice on how to make one meal the whole family will love.

My suggestions for breakfasts, main meals, dips and desserts, as well as a handful of nourishing snacks, are the foods I enjoy with my family. But in truth, sometimes dinner at our house is a boiled egg with some buttered sourdough toast, and a quick bowl of plain yoghurt, berries and a sprinkle of seeds. This is OK and, quite frankly, this is life. As long as you are choosing from a good foundation of real foods, nature will take care of the rest.

'Eat food. Not too much. Mostly plants.'

• Michael Pollan, author, journalist and activist

Time to *Begin*

The pace of a baby's development over their first few months of life almost seems to defy logic.

As they move rapidly from one milestone to the next, there's barely any time for you to complete their baby book (that's my excuse, anyway). Before you know it, the time has come to gradually wean them onto foods. Or at least you think it has. How exactly are you supposed to know when to start?

From a purely nutritional perspective, the World Health Organization (WHO) reassures us that the nutrient stores with which a baby is born, as well as exclusive breastfeeding, should provide adequate nutrition for the first 6 months. There are a couple of exceptions: vitamin K, of which babies receive an injection shortly after birth, and vitamin D, which breastfeeding mothers are advised to take as a supplement. If a baby seems hungrier at any time before this – possibly indicative of a growth spurt – extra breast milk (or infant formula) should be enough to meet their needs.

Now, clearly nothing magical happens overnight when a baby turns 6 months old (unless perhaps they sleep through uninterrupted), and so there is often some debate as to whether the 6-month mark is best for all babies.

Certainly we know that we don't want to delay beyond this point. Nutritional requirements gradually increase at this time, in part because a baby's stores of some nutrients have now wound down and breast milk (or infant formula) is no longer enough. But also, we don't want to miss out on the window for safely introducing food allergens (see page 53).

As we don't want weaning to become a science experiment or regimented like a military exercise, I'd suggest looking to your own baby for the signs that they are ready to begin. If that's a little earlier than 6 months, research suggests no significant benefits or drawbacks to starting slightly earlier. The key here is when I say 'ready to begin'. What I mean is ready to begin feeding themselves, which, fortuitously, happens for most babies at 6 months, or thereabouts (nature is clever like that).

Self-feeding

While 'traditional' weaning guidelines advocate a parent-led approach, with a gradual shift from puréed to lumpy to normal textures where a baby is fed from a spoon, there is an alternative way called 'baby-led weaning' (BLW), where a baby is in control of feeding themselves. Although this may sound radical, I can assure you it's not. Most 6-month-olds are entirely capable of picking up food and putting it – and many other things that take their fancy, for that matter – in their mouths.

In actual fact, introducing 'finger foods' at 6 months alongside spoonfeeding is already recommended by a number of public health organisations – for instance, the UK Department of Health, the American Academy of Pediatrics, and Health Canada. The only difference between these official guidelines and BLW is that a baby is not being spoonfed at all, just self-fed.

Self-feeding seems to me a much more intuitive way for a baby to learn about food, and presents a number of potential benefits.

'Spoonfeeding in the long run teaches us nothing but the shape of the spoon.'

• E. M. Forster, author

⁕ PERCEPTION

Self-feeding enables a baby to tune in to their feelings of appetite, hunger and fullness, set their own pace at mealtimes and retain control of what and how much they eat. This clever appetite monitor is incredibly important in ensuring nutrient needs are met, not exceeded, and is something that gets a bit rusty as we get older.

On the other hand, if someone else is doing the feeding, they'll have no way of gauging these internal cues and may run the risk of overriding them. Of course, in such cases, some more wilful babies may clamp their mouth shut, turn their head away or spit the food back out, but none of these options seems particularly conducive to a pleasant eating experience.

⁕ FAMILIARISATION

We've already talked about the important role that familiarisation plays in establishing our food preferences and, with that in mind, it seems completely counterintuitive to me to hide what a baby is eating by blitzing it into an unrecognisable mush. Even more so if that mush is being consumed straight from a pouch, where a baby can't even see it.

Research shows that, with both new tastes and textures, babies are more receptive in the earlier months of weaning and that this tails off over time. In this way, failing to make the most of those open-minded early experiences feels like a missed opportunity.

Now, to be clear, I'm not the purée police. I have nothing against puréeing per se. Indeed, my food processor would be the one kitchen appliance I would pack to take to my elusive desert island (along with a solar-powered battery pack for it, of course). I purée lots of things: soups, nut butters, smoothies, dressings and so on. And this book is not without recipes for these. The point I'm making is that mush isn't the sole focus; rather, real, whole, recognisable food is, and I believe it should serve as the basis for food learning.

⋙ OBSERVATION

Babies and children learn many things by watching others and imitating them. When a whole family sits down to share the same meal, this further reinforces to curious beginners what's safe and acceptable to eat. I'll have what they're having, so to speak.

⋙ PREPARATION

Although babies and children are more willing to accept very soft foods that they can deal with easily (we'd all prefer an easier life), if we don't introduce suitably textured foods, babies will have less opportunity to achieve sufficient training and exercise to support their early motor development.

For instance, in the ALSPAC study (see page 12), researchers found that delaying the introduction of lumpy foods beyond 9 months was linked to more feeding problems, both in the short term and at their seven-year follow up.

As with any training, the greater the opportunity to practise, the better babies will get and the easier and more effortless it will become for them to deal with challenging textures, which in turn should lead to liking.

That's not to say we can go ahead introducing any old food at 6 months – babies at this age aren't equipped to deal with everything we'd eat as adults. It can be a couple of years until a baby has a mouth full of teeth and the strength and coordination to deal with harder solids, and even then some foods such as whole nuts still present a choking risk. Nonetheless, the vast majority of family foods can be adapted in some way for self-feeding babies, and I'll endeavour to show you how through the recipes in this book.

⋙ SIGNS OF READINESS

- Able to sit comfortably with little or no help, thereby freeing up their hands instead of using them for balance

- Able to reach for and grasp objects

My tried-and-tested method of knowing whether babies are ready to start feeding themselves is involving them in mealtimes (hopefully by now you're managing to make time, rather than eating on the fly, if at all). When they're steady enough that they are not going to wobble off or head-butt the table, sit them on your lap and watch what they do.

To begin with they may just observe the whole process open-mouthed, in wonderment. But once you see them purposefully reach forwards to pick up something off your plate and smoothly and confidently bring it up to their mouth, you'll know that they are probably ready to begin.

How to begin

This may sound odd, but in the very early days ensure that your baby isn't hungry at mealtimes. This is because they won't yet have acquired the self-feeding skills necessary to eat enough to match their appetite, and this could lead to an irritated baby. Instead, satisfy their hunger with breast- or bottle-feeding initially, while they get to grips with developing the skills they need.

When following a self-feeding approach, we need to think about what to offer that is easy for a baby to pick up and handle, as well as what are they can swallow safely.

The term 'finger food' is often used to describe the best size and shape for handling in the first few months – in other words, long and thin, such as a stick of cucumber or a toast 'soldier'. This shape is effective because it enables a baby to hold on to one half of the 'finger' and place the other half in their mouth.

As they don't yet have the dexterity to open their fist, a baby would otherwise get a small piece of food trapped and squished between their fingers and palm – much to their annoyance and puzzlement. Over time, and given ample opportunity, they do get better at this, gradually moving on to smaller and more irregular shapes.

We also need to consider the firmness of food. The knack with this is to offer foods that will not break up when a learner baby misjudges their grip and squeezes too much, but also ones that will not pose a choking risk.

At 6 months, most babies will sprout their first tooth and signal the onset of the delightful phase of teething – a painfully slow and drawn-out process that may last until their third birthday. Fortunately, toothless little ones can do a good deal of munching with just their gums. Our jaw muscles are incredibly powerful – the strongest muscles in our body, in fact. You can test food to check whether it's suitable by using your tongue to push it up against the roof of your mouth and see whether it's soft enough to break down without using your teeth.

By around 9 months, most babies will have progressed to a pincer grip, picking up small pieces of food between their thumb and forefinger. This is a natural safety mechanism, allowing a baby's skills in handling smaller food to develop in tandem with their ability to swallow it safely.

Examples of soft starter finger foods

- Soft fruit pieces such as banana, kiwi fruit, orange segments (remove any pips), very ripe peach or pear
- Cooked (baked, roast, steamed, boiled) vegetable sticks such as carrot, zucchini (courgette), parsnip, sweet potato
- Cooked vegetable pieces such as broccoli or cauliflower florets
- Cooked pasta
- Slow-cooked strips of meat or poultry
- Omelette strips
- Bread or toast 'soldiers'

A couple of pointers: babies are using their hands, so always remember to allow enough time for food to cool properly. And perhaps a less obvious one, you may want your little one to master the art of naked banana eating because soft banana (a favourite first food to try with BLW) is a nightmare to get out of clothes.

Things to be mindful of

First and foremost, it's very important that a baby or child is never left unattended when eating, and that they are not distracted or leaning back in their seat. And while it's completely natural to worry that they may not be eating enough, resist the urge to put any pressure on them to hurry or clear their plate, and certainly never put whole pieces of food directly into their mouth. A baby should retain complete control at all times. A parent's role is simply to ensure that mealtimes are nutritious and safe, and to offer support where necessary, such as nudging the broccoli a little closer if it is flicked out of reach.

In the early days of weaning, it's quite likely that a baby will gag on some foods. This is nothing to panic about or be put off by, although I do appreciate (having been there on more than one occasion) how hard it is to keep calm when it does happen.

Gagging is different from choking. It is very common among all babies, regardless of how they are weaned, and is a necessary part of their learning process. A baby's gag reflex is triggered further forwards than an adult's, thereby offering greater protection of the airway (another of nature's safety mechanisms), but this also means that it will be activated more easily.

When the gag reflex is triggered, it aims to bring large pieces of food forwards for further chewing. Be patient and calm, and a baby will usually cough it forwards after a few attempts. By the time a baby is around age of 8 or 9 months, the gag reflex will have moved further back in the mouth, and those hairy gagging moments will happen less frequently from thereon in.

> *A baby should retain complete control at all times. A parent's role is simply to ensure mealtimes are nutritious and safe, and offer support ...*

Choking, on the other hand, happens when an object such as food gets lodged in the throat and obstructs the flow of air. If this happens a baby will be unable to breathe or make any noise, and parents must act quickly to dislodge the food. Never try to remove food by putting your fingers into the mouth, as this may push it further down. Recommended first aid involves supporting the baby face-down on your thigh and administering five back blows; if this is unsuccessful follow up with five chest thrusts. Instructions and videos for how to do this are widely available online, and a paediatric first-aid course is a good idea for any new parent.

Foods with a high risk of choking

- Grapes, cherries, cherry tomatoes

- Hard raw fruit or vegetables such as diced apple, carrot, celery

- Small, hard vegetables such as fresh green peas or sweetcorn kernels

- Chunks of cheese

- Whole nuts and large seeds

- 'Claggy' nut butter such as peanut butter given on a spoon – thinly spread on toast is fine

- Round, coin-sized foods

- Corn chips, crackers, popcorn, potato crisps (potato chips)*

- Sausages*

- Confectionery (candy)*

* These foods are also not recommended due to their poor nutritional content.

Food hygiene tips

Wash your hands before preparing food and your baby's hands before they eat.

✕

Ensure any plates, bowls, cups, cutlery, utensils, equipment and work surfaces are clean before using, but there's no need to sterilise.

✕

Use separate chopping boards and utensils for preparing raw and cooked foods.

✕

Wash all fruit and vegetables well before preparing.

✕

Store freshly cooked food for up to 24 hours in a sealed container in the refrigerator.

✕

Ensure reheated food is piping hot all the way through, then cooled before feeding. Don't reheat food more than once.

✕

Thaw frozen food in the refrigerator, and don't refreeze.

Creating the right space

Establishing the right environment for mealtimes is just as important as thinking about what foods to offer. BLW forms part of a practice called 'responsive feeding', which means allowing babies and children to eat at their own pace – bearing in mind that with beginners this can be very slow. It's also about supporting and encouraging them to eat their food, without ever forcing them or resorting to bribes.

Be aware that a baby's facial expression may not match what they're actually feeling, and if they pull a face of dislike, even if repeatedly, this could mean 'I'm not sure what this is' rather than 'I don't like this'. Likewise, although a baby may pause for a time and may even start playfully throwing food on the floor, this does not necessarily mean that they've finished their meal. They may just be taking a break to explore – wait a few more minutes to see.

This brings me to the point that, to retain any sanity, you're going to have to embrace the mess that ensues with BLW and accept that, unless you have a dog, there'll be some wastage. I found that my second baby, Jonathan, would systematically throw everything off his highchair and onto the floor, until he was left with one morsel of food to concentrate on exclusively. Babies are easily overwhelmed and easily distracted.

I've found the best way to minimise any carnage is to offer a small number of foods of different tastes and textures for a baby to choose from, without going overboard, and to keep a warm, clean cloth to hand. Using a plate, even the 'suction' style ones, can eventually send food flying at the wall, and just creates extra washing up. So see how you go with just using their highchair as a surface for them to eat from in the first few months. Lastly, if you don't have a floor that can be wiped over easily, be sure to cover the carpet, rug or the like with an oilcloth or something similar.

Nourishing
Foundations

I believe that the problem with modern diets is largely that we have lost perspective as to what it means to have balance.

We are so overwhelmed by an environment of ultra-processed foods that these have infiltrated our lives and become the mainstay of our diets, without so much as a second thought. These 'foods' either push out or are eaten as well as the simple, wholesome foods that our bodies need to be healthy, and we all suffer as a result.

Sadly, the pursuit of a wholesome diet has come to be seen as a sort of purist, hippie affair, reserved only for those who have the time and money, as well as a big kitchen, a vegetable patch and perhaps some chickens thrown in for good measure. There also seems to be a sense that eating well means compromising on taste and enjoyment, and somehow strips the life and joy from food. Nothing could be further from the truth, of course. I hope, through my snippets of know-how and recipes, to foster and inspire a love of real food. A true love, one where children eat their leaves only because they enjoy them – not because they think they have to.

Wholefood, plant-based

What we eat not only has a bearing on how healthy we are, but impacts the health of our planet and its ability to sustain us now and into the future as well. It's no exaggeration that our current food system is devastating our planet, and it's critical that eating well is also about being respectful of environmental limits.

The biggest thing we can do to ensure our diets are more sustainable is to base them on plants. We do not need to become vegan; rather, the majority of what we eat should have come directly from the earth. The savings we make from doing this can then go towards smaller amounts of sustainably produced meat, eggs and dairy foods.

Organic farming has been shown to be more sustainable than conventional farming. There is also sound evidence that organic foods are more nutritious, although there is often debate as to whether the small gains are meaningful across the whole diet. Nevertheless, the American Academy of Pediatrics advocates organic foods wherever possible, to reduce children's exposure to pesticides and drug-resistant bacteria (as organically raised animals have tighter controls on the use of antibiotics). We should also be mindful of following nature's rhythm and making use of foods only when they're in season. Fresher food tastes better, is more nutritious and is kinder on our purse. Support nearby farmers and cut food miles by choosing locally grown whenever possible. Finally, avoid over-packaged foods, especially if the packaging can't be recycled.

Foundation foods

A nourishing diet that supports the needs of a rapidly growing baby or child – one grounded in nutrient-rich, wholesome foods – is beneficial for the entire family. Still, we need to be mindful of some aspects of early life nutrition, so that we provide the right balance of foods to nurture little ones and ensure that they thrive.

Sorting foods according to the nutrients they provide gives us five foundation food groups:

- whole grains

- vegetables

- legumes, nuts, seeds, eggs, fish, poultry and red meat

- dairy foods (milk, yoghurt, cheese) and plant-based alternatives

- fruit.

Offering a good mix of foods in each of these groups, in roughly the proportions shown here, is what we mean when we say a balanced diet. There's no need to overthink this and meet these exact amounts at every single meal, or even every day. We can store many nutrients, and there's a level of crossover between the groups in terms of what they provide. Think of it instead as a general guide to how our diets should look over time.

Dairy foods & plant-based alternatives

Legumes, nuts, seeds, eggs, fish, poultry & red meat

Fruit

quinoa

pasta

oats

Vegetables

Whole grains

Plant-based fats

olive oil

Weaning without borders: 6–12 months

I remember Laurence's first foray into food. He sucked on a lemon that I'd been zesting for a cake and, quite surprisingly to me, after an initial wince he went back for more!

Babies will surprise you with what they will eat. Humans are omnivores, after all, and we come pre-programmed to seek out and enjoy a huge variety of foods to meet our nutritional requirements. There's no need to shy away from light spices or bitter, sour or other strong flavours, nor is it necessary to follow some sort of preordained pathway where food A must precede food B by precisely four days. Weaning is not a science experiment.

There are very few restrictions in terms of what not to offer when you start weaning – namely, those foods that present a choking risk, and honey because of the risk of botulism. And while it's quite common to see advice to introduce foods one at a time, to spot those that may cause some sort of reaction, the reality is that only a very small number of babies are affected by food hypersensitivities and in using this approach it would literally take months to introduce a range of foods conducive to a balanced diet.

So let's crack on with offering safe and nutritious first foods, using your usual family foods as a guide, and adapting them as necessary to match your baby's self-feeding skills. Remember, too, that your baby's tummy is still very small and that they'll need small amounts of food, more often.

Growing up whole: 12 months onwards

By around 12 months, a baby's food intake and meal patterns will more closely resemble those of the rest of the family. Their self-feeding skills will be well honed by now, aided by a few teeth and a basic, coordinated chewing technique.

Continue to offer food regularly – at 12 months a pattern of three meals and two or three snacks will be likely. Be mindful that the purpose of this rhythm is to present an opportunity to eat, so that little ones don't get too hungry and frustrated. It's not to force them into having food because you feel that they need it. Babies have much better appetite control than we do as adults, and we can support them in tuning in to their own bodies, rather than overriding their internal cues for the sake of routine.

For this reason, I've also avoided giving specific portion sizes. You'll notice that in the recipes I give a general guide of a baby's portion being half that of an adult's – but the amounts that little ones will eat can vary considerably from one meal to the next and one day to the next. Provided you are offering them a range of foods from each of the five food groups and they seem to be growing well and thriving, you don't give too much thought to how much is going in them versus how much is landing on the floor.

Equally, from around this time you may also begin to notice that your once-adventurous baby who would eat whatever you offered them becomes a more cautious toddler – at least where food is concerned. They may be more hesitant to try new foods or even snub foods that they've previously enjoyed. Stay calm. This is all part of their natural development and is completely normal.

Indeed, I often think that labelling this stage 'fussy eating' puts a negative spin on something that's actually a positive. From an evolutionary perspective, exercising such caution would have prevented newly mobile toddlers from inadvertently harming themselves by eating random things they came across. Moreover, developing a sense of self and autonomy is so important in little ones – an attribute to nurture, rather than despair at.

So how can we foster healthy eating when we come up against such resistance? Well, the best thing is to do is be persistent and consistent in offering healthy foods. This stage usually peaks somewhere around 18–24 months and then drops off, although all children are different.

A European study of more than 300 preschool children aged between 4 and 38 months looked at how they responded to being repeatedly offered artichoke. From this, they were then grouped according to how their liking of it changed:

- 'Plate-clearers' (21%) needed little persuading and were in artichoke heaven.

- 'Learners' (40%) gradually increased their intake over time.

- 'Non-eaters' (16%) kept their mouths clamped shut.

- 'Others' (23%) didn't really fit into one of the groups above, probably being quite promiscuous in their eating behaviour.

You can see that most of the children fell into the learner category, which I think reinforces that persistence with offering foods can pay off over time. Of those at the extremes, the plate-clearers were more likely to be younger, and the stubborn non-eaters were more likely to be older – highlighting that, when it comes to instilling healthier food habits, the earlier the better:

- Cultivate a pleasant mealtime environment, one that's calm and free of distractions, and not rushed. Where possible, sit down together and share the same meal.

- Offer a variety of nutritious foods from all of the foundation food groups.

- Offer new foods with familiar ones – you may be surprised at what children will eat if given the chance. Remember, it is the number of times they taste the new foods rather than the amount they have that will ultimately drive a liking for them. For some, it may take upwards of ten tries.

- Be positive and offer praise as a reward, rather than being coercive and using other foods as a bribe – 'If you eat this you can have that.'

Offer new foods with familiar ones – you may be surprised at what children will eat if given the chance.

But first, milk

Without doubt, breast milk (or infant formula) continues to make a vital contribution to a baby's nutritional intake well past their first birthday. That said, milk should be only a base, providing about half of their needs from 6 to 12 months and a third from 12 to 24 months. As we gradually introduce solid foods, these need to be replete in nutrients, with equal if not more energy than the breast milk (or infant formula) they're replacing, to ensure that there's no shortfall.

On a side note, parents sometimes start weaning early (by 'early' we mean before a baby can self-feed) because they're concerned that their baby's appetite is not being satisfied through breast milk (or infant formula) alone. Fruit and vegetable purées would be typical first foods. While homemade fruit and vegetable purées can be nutritious, they're also low in energy and on their own are not going deliver some sort of nutritional panacea.

Breastfed babies who are fed on demand will progressively reduce their intake of breast milk to balance the extra nourishment they get from foods. Formula-fed babies will need to do the same, and they can be supported by being offered less formula and not encouraged to finish the bottle.

It's important to be sensitive to a baby's needs. On some days they may want more formula than on others, especially if they're feeling under the weather. As a guide, 7- to 9-month-olds will have about 600 ml (21 fl oz) of formula a day – usually on waking, before naps and bedtime; by 10–12 months this drops to about 400 ml (14 fl oz) per day, and this amount may continue for the next couple of years.

When we first start weaning, there is no need to worry too much about the spacing of feeds around meals (no one wants a hungry baby getting frustrated because they can't self-feed well enough yet). As the weeks progress, feeds shouldn't be given too close to meals, to encourage an appetite for solid foods. For example, around the 9-month mark, you may think about dropping their early morning feed to encourage breakfast, then offer a 'top-up' feed afterwards.

OTHER FLUIDS

Infants need nothing more to drink than breast milk (or infant formula) and water from 6 to 12 months. Offer a cup of water with each meal and snack from 6 months onwards, and where possible encourage your baby to sip from a cup with your support. If you do want to use a lidded cup, look for ones that are 'free flow' if possible, They'll result in a bit more spillage in the short term, but will teach sipping rather than sucking. By about 12 months, babies have generally mastered the art of sipping and can gently be weaned off their bottle and onto cups for all fluids.

Throughout this book I have not specified what type of milk should be used in recipes, unless it's particularly important to the flavour. Go ahead and use whichever milk you prefer. All recipes have been tested with cow's and soya milk; other, more watery milks such as almond or oat milk may need their volume adjusted slightly. From about 12 months onwards, full-fat animal or calcium-fortified unsweetened plant-based milks can be used as drinks in place of infant formula. Just be mindful that these are usually lower in fat than cow's milk, and ensure that you compensate with other foods. Note also that rice milk or rice drinks shouldn't be given until at least 5 years of age because they contain small amounts of arsenic.

As for everything else … fruit juice, squashes and sugary or artificially sweetened carbonated drinks are completely unnecessary and may encourage a preference for these over water – which can be a stubborn habit to break. If you do offer fruit juice, make sure that it's well diluted, only given at mealtimes and only once a day. Finally, the only people drinking tea and coffee should be the tired parents. Tea and coffee contain not only caffeine, but also nutrient blockers that prevent the absorption of iron.

Key nutrients and health concerns

It's not necessary to have a degree in nutritional science to eat well. Humankind managed to thrive for thousands of years without knowing that vitamins even existed. Still, a brief overview of some

of the nutrients we're particularly concerned about in early years will help you to feel confident that you have a measured approach to things such as sugars, sodium and iron. I'll also walk you through some of the issues you may come across on your new food adventure with your little one, such as food allergies and tummy troubles.

FATS

Fats provide a concentrated source of energy, and are therefore an important part of the diets of little ones. They help them to meet their nutritional needs for supporting their colossal growth and development. Fats also supply important building materials for cell membranes, brain matter and hormones, to name but a few, and they carry crucial fat-soluble vitamins.

The different types of fats in our diets are usually lumped into three main groups: saturated, polyunsaturated and monounsaturated. Foods do not contain just one fat from these three groups, but rather a mixture. Animals foods are generally higher in saturated fats than plant foods (although coconut oil is a rare exception), and plant foods are higher in polyunsaturated and monounsaturated fats. Both poly- and monounsaturated fats are known to be most beneficial in terms of heart health; however, modern diets are usually tipped too far the other way, and people get too much saturated fat.

You may also have heard of omega-3 and omega-6 fats. These belong to the polyunsaturated fat group, and they are essential fats because our bodies can't make them. Although supplements of these essential fats are often touted, particularly for little ones, there is no compelling research to suggest that a varied and balanced diet can't supply all the essential fats we need. For example, omega-3s are found in oily fish and, in lesser amounts, in grass-fed red meat, poultry and eggs.

In addition, all plant foods contain an omega-3 fat called ALA. Nuts, seeds and their oils are the best sources, particularly linseed (flaxseeds), chia seeds and walnuts. Plant-based omega-3s are often dismissed as being inferior to those from animal sources,

Fats provide a concentrated source of energy, and are therefore an important part of the diets of little ones. They help them to meet their nutritional needs for supporting their colossal growth and development.

particularly oily fish, but vegetarians and vegans – who have limited, if any, animal-source omega-3s in their diets – show no signs of deficiency in essential fats.

Finally, added fats, just like added sugars, can quickly ramp up the energy content of foods, so we need to be mindful of using small amounts of added fats in our cooking. That said, babies and toddlers have particularly high energy needs and so they shouldn't be eating 'low-fat' foods. In short, ensure that most of their fats come from wholefood plant sources.

PROTEIN

We need proteins to grow and maintain all the cells in the body, and we need more during periods of growth, such as our early years. Proteins are made of building blocks called amino acids. Some of these we can make ourselves, and others we can get only from our diets. These are called essential amino acids and, while animal foods contain all the essential amino acids, plant foods on their own often don't (except soya beans, quinoa, buckwheat, amaranth, hempseeds and chia seeds). Including a wide variety of foods in the diet ensures that any gaps are filled, even in vegan diets.

CARBOHYDRATES

Carbohydrates are broadly grouped into sugars, starches and fibre, and they provide us with most of the energy in our diets. The speed with which carbohydrate-containing foods are digested and absorbed is known as the glycemic index (GI); a lower GI indicates that the carbohydrate is digested and absorbed more slowly, and therefore is easier for the body to deal with. Generally speaking, wholefoods have a lower GI than ultra-processed foods.

SUGARS

Simple sugars that are on their own – in other words, not linked together to make starches – are naturally found in a wide range of foods, such as fruit, milk and honey. We're perfectly able to deal

Looking after teeth

You can start brushing teeth as soon as a baby's first teeth
pop up. Use a small, soft-bristled child-sized toothbrush with
a smear of children's toothpaste. You may find it easier
to do this from behind to begin with.

with modest amounts of sugars as part of a wholefood diet, and our
bodies, particularly our brains, use them as a source of energy. As
with all things that we eat, though, too much sugar, too often, can
cause harm.

First, think about the extra sugars that are added to foods, such as
table sugar, honey and syrups. All these, even those that are less
refined, such as honey or maple syrup, add additional calories with
negligible if any beneficial nutrients. These 'empty calories' can
quickly ramp up our energy intake, which, if not used, will lead
to weight gain. Added sugars can also displace more nutritious
foods from our diet; although our energy needs may be met our
nutrient needs are not. For babies and children, this means that
their development will be compromised.

Secondly, the bacteria in our mouths love feeding off simple sugars,
and regularly providing them with their favourite food can lead
to the development of plaque and dental decay. Dental caries is
a huge issue for children nowadays, with estimates that around
half of school-aged children have decay in at least one tooth.

In terms of dental health, it matters less whether the sugars are
naturally present or added – chemically speaking, they're the same
and the bacteria are not fussy. For instance, the sucrose in table
sugar is the same as the sucrose in fruit. What's more relevant is how

often we feed the plaque bacteria, particularly as we need to leave plenty of space in the day for our bodies to clean and restore balance in our mouth after eating. So, for example, frequent sugary snacks between meals or drinking a sugary drink over, say, 30 minutes, will send plaque bacteria into overdrive.

None of this means that the sugars contained in wholefoods such as fruit are some sort of food foe. On the contrary, fruit provides a whole host of beneficial nutrients along with its sugar content, and it's very hard to go overboard with the amount of fruit in our diet when we eat fruits in their whole form. What this does mean is that fruit is best kept to mealtimes.

Finally, it's important that we keep the sugars added to food in check, so that we don't push out more beneficial foods. I use added sugars incredibly sparingly and prefer instead to sweeten recipes using fruit in their whole or dried form – providing ample nutrients along with their sweetness. None of the recipes in this book is overly sweet in itself, relying instead on the intrinsic sweetness of ingredients such as coconut, vanilla and cinnamon.

SODIUM/SALT

Sodium is an essential nutrient at all stages of life, playing an important role in fluid balance and maintaining our blood pressure. Too much sodium in our blood, however, can hold on to water, increasing our blood pressure and giving our heart extra work to do. In the long run this can increase our risk of heart disease and stroke.

To reduce the burden of excess sodium, our body excretes some when we urinate, but the immature kidneys of babies are not at all effective at doing this. What's more, studies show that the inclusion of salty foods during weaning can drive a preference for saltier foods later on – another example of how our early food choices can have an impact in the long run. As a result, it's especially important to limit the amount of sodium in the diets of little ones, which means not adding salt (sodium chloride) during preparation, cooking or at the table, and being careful to use salt-containing ingredients frugally:

- Babies aged less than 12 months should have no more than 0.2 g (200 mg) sodium (500 mg salt) per day.

- Toddlers aged from 1 to 3 years should have no more than 0.4 g (400 mg) sodium (1000 mg salt) per day.

Checking the label is really the only way to gauge how much sodium/salt is found in a product. As a guide, looking at the amount of sodium/salt per 100 g can tell you whether a product is high in these or not, and this figure is useful when comparing similar products. But also take a look at the amount of sodium/salt per serving and consider what that means for a baby or child. It's surprising how quickly the numbers tot up; for example, a single slice of bread could contain 0.2 g (200 mg) sodium (500 mg salt).

Low sodium = less than 0.1 g (100 mg) per 100 g (300 mg salt)
High sodium = more than 0.6 g (600 mg) per 100 g (1500 mg salt)

IRON

Iron is an essential mineral that plays a multitude of roles, but most notably it carries oxygen in our blood and around the body. It is unquestionably fundamental to good health, and the amount of it available to use is controlled by how much we absorb from food.

So, for example, during pregnancy and breastfeeding, when our requirements for iron increase, our bodies will go ahead and absorb more iron from our food (this increase in efficiency of absorbing nutrients when pregnant is one of the reasons why you, sadly, do not need to eat for two). Likewise, when we have all the iron we need, we will absorb less.

Iron deficiency is the most common micronutrient deficiency in the world and is believed to be surprisingly widespread in babies and toddlers, where it can have a permanent, negative impact on their physical and mental development. Symptoms of iron deficiency include tiredness and pallor, but these are easily missed or dismissed as being due to other things.

The amount of iron needed by babies and children is relatively high, to support their rapid growth. Full-term babies should have enough iron stores to see them safely through the first 6 months, especially if there was a delay in clamping the umbilical cord until it stopped pulsing. But from then on, extra iron is needed, and it's vital that we provide plenty through diet. As a guide, I recommend including at least one iron-rich food as part of each meal.

Iron is found in two forms in food: haem iron, which is well absorbed and is found almost exclusively red meat, fish and poultry, and non-haem iron, which is less well absorbed and is also found in red meat, poultry and fish, but in grains, legumes, leafy green vegetables and eggs as well.

A number of dietary factors can increase the absorption of non-haem iron, such as vitamin C (found in fruit and vegetables), and there are those that hinder absorption, such as phytates (found in grains, nuts, seeds and legumes). I really wouldn't get too bogged down in the detail of what does what, though, because with a varied and balanced diet they'll more or less cancel each other out.

Through the recipes in this book I encourage plenty of plants (providing non-haem iron and vitamin C), along with some red meat, fish and poultry (a little haem iron helps non-haem iron absorption), and there are some simple examples of how you can reduce phytates in grains by soaking and fermenting them overnight.

While we're talking about plants, it is worth noting that, although concerns are sometimes voiced about the iron content of vegetarian diets being low, studies show that broadly speaking there is no increased risk of iron deficiency if the diet is varied and balanced.

VITAMIN D

Vitamin D is a bit of an oddity of the nutrient world because we get only very small amounts of it from a limited number of natural food sources, such as oily fish, meat and eggs. The sun shining on our skin supplies most of our vitamin D; if exposure is insufficient, supplements are recommended. Ensuring adequate vitamin D in infancy and early childhood is especially important because it's needed to support rapid bone growth.

Whether or not your little one will need a vitamin D supplement depends on whether they're at risk of low vitamin D levels. For example, in the United Kingdom, which is a bit of a trek from the equator, vitamin D is made only from April to September, and so it is recommended that all babies and children up to 5 years of age take a supplement. Australia is fortunate enough to get a smidge more sunshine, so there is no blanket recommendation for everyone, and this is also the case in Canada and the United States. Only those who are at higher risk should have a daily vitamin D supplement of 400 IU (10µg).

People at risk of vitamin D deficiency would include those with very dark skin or those who don't expose their skin to the sun, through either staying indoors or covered. Breastfed babies can be at an increased risk if their mother had low vitamin D levels during pregnancy and therefore provided her baby with only a small store of the vitamin at birth (breast milk is low in vitamin D). Experts think that we probably still make enough vitamin D when we have sunscreen on as protection against harmful UV rays, and sun safety should never be compromised.

DIETARY SUPPLEMENTS

People with varied and balanced omnivorous diets don't usually need supplements. Nevertheless, some countries do recommend targeted supplements because dietary surveys may have shown nutritional gaps that need plugging. For instance, the UK Department of Health has recommended supplements of vitamins A, C and D from 6 months to 5 years old, and vitamin D for breastfeeding mothers from when the baby is born.

Check your government's health department website to see what their official advice is, and be mindful of how that may apply to your little one. For example, although supplements may not be generally recommended (as is the case in Australia), if you have concerns about nutritional intake (perhaps during illness or if you're grappling with a period of picky eating), they can be a good idea at these times. Your health professional can offer advice if needed.

If you do decide to use supplements, consider using drops or sprays rather than 'gummies', which I think can send a confusing message to little ones by introducing 'occasional' foods on a daily basis.

Growing well

Monitoring growth is one of the best ways to know whether little ones are getting enough nutrition. This is generally done by your health professional at check-ups, when they'll plot measurements of weight, length/height, head circumference and sometimes body mass index (BMI) on what we call centile charts. These charts are based on measurements of healthy growth in full-term babies that were exclusively or predominantly breastfed for the first 4–6 months.

There's no ideal spot to be on a centile chart, although those babies and children at the edges may sometimes be monitored more closely (and those off the chart, so to speak, certainly). The simple way to explain how they work is, if 100 little ones of the same age stood or lay side by side in a line in order of their weight, height, head circumference or BMI, the fiftieth centile would be the fiftieth and middle baby or child – all those on one side would be heavier, taller and so on, and on the other side, lighter and shorter.

My only caveat to this is that looking at one point in time doesn't give the whole picture. The key is looking at how growth tracks over time, as normal growth naturally follows the centile line, or runs parallel to it in the centile space (the bit between the lines). A little bit of fluctuation here and there would be normal – we're not robots, after all. Little ones may also lose a little weight if they're ill for a time, then regain it when their appetite improves. It's also worth noting that it's not of great concern if they're not on the same centile for weight and height.

Vegetarianism

Outlined below are some vegetarian and vegan wholefood sources of key nutrients that we're particularly concerned about in the diets of babies and children. Fortified options such as plant-based milks (calcium) and nutritional yeast (vitamin B12) can also be helpful. There are plenty of choices for a nourishing plant-based diet.

Nutrient	Wholefood sources	Notes
Omega-3 fats	Linseeds (flaxseeds) (whole, ground, oil), hempseeds (whole, ground, oil), chia seeds (whole, ground, oil), canola/rapeseed oil, soya beans, tofu, walnuts, sweet potato, pepitas (pumpkin seeds), leafy green vegetables	Include at least once a day with a vegan diet
Protein	Eggs, dairy foods, beans, pulses, lentils, nuts and nut butters, seeds and seed butters, tofu, grains	
Vitamin B12	Dairy foods, eggs	As vitamin B12 is not found naturally in plant foods, it can be completely missing from vegan diets. Vegan mothers who are breastfeeding should ensure that they get enough vitamin B12 from fortified foods and/or a supplement. From 6 months onwards, vegans will need to have fortified products or a B12 supplement to meet their requirements
Vitamin D	Eggs	See section on vitamin D (page 46) and dietary supplements for further information
Calcium	Dairy foods, green vegetables (broccoli, cabbage, collard greens, bok choy [pak choy], turnip greens, kale), dried figs, almonds (whole, ground, butter), tahini	
Iron	Dairy foods, soya beans, tofu, tempeh, cooked legumes (lentils, chickpeas, adzuki, kidney), pepitas (pumpkin seeds), cashews, sunflower seeds, tahini, baked potatoes with skin on	
Zinc	Soya beans, tofu, baked beans, lentils, pepitas (pumpkin seeds), cashews, sunflower seeds, cooked peas	

It's entirely possible for a vegetarian diet devoid of meat and fish, but including eggs and dairy foods, to meet all the nutritional needs to support optimal growth and development in babies and children. Indeed, advice on what to offer, in terms of a good variety of foods, doesn't differ at all from omnivorous diets.

That said, some nutrients, such as iron, essential omega-3 fats and protein, are better absorbed or more complete in animal sources, meaning that it's easier to meet nutritional requirements by including them, even in small amounts. Vegetarians (and vegans) therefore need to be a bit more mindful of ensuring that a good variety of foods across all five food groups is consumed.

Veganism

While veganism does present a greater risk of nutritional deficiencies, it's possible for a well-planned vegan diet – that is, one devoid of all animal products, including dairy, eggs and honey – to provide sufficient nutrients for growth and development. The only exception to this is vitamin B12, which is found exclusively in animal foods.

It's also generally advised that little vegans be breastfed for as long as possible – ideally two years or longer – to meet nutritional requirements. Those who are partially breastfed (or have infant formula) will benefit from continuing with a soya-based infant formula for their first two years. Other preparations, including unmodified plant-based milks such as soy, rice, almond or coconut or homemade formulas, should not be used in place of breast milk (or infant formula). It's worth seeking advice from a dietitian if you plan to raise your little one on a vegan diet.

Food hypersensitivities

On rare occasions, babies and children may experience unpleasant, sometimes life-threatening reactions after eating a certain food. We call these food hypersensitivities, a term covering a broad spectrum of issues, including allergies, intolerances and coeliac disease.

It's really important, if you suspect a food hypersensitivity, that you stop offering the culprit food, but don't self-diagnose. There is a considerable amount of overlap in the symptoms of food hypersensitivities. For example, diarrhoea after consuming cow's milk could be down to an allergy to cow's milk protein or a malabsorption of lactose – the sugar in milk – or both. And they are treated differently. Always seek advice from a doctor with experience in this area before reintroducing the food, or before cutting it out indefinitely – which can compromise the nutritional content of your child's diet.

On a side note, remember that the facial skin of babies is very sensitive. Many foods, including the acidic juices of citrus, tomatoes and berries, may irritate the skin and cause redness. This isn't food hypersensitivity and doesn't mean that you need to cut these foods out of your baby's diet.

Food allergies

Food allergies occur when the immune system mistakes something that has been eaten as dangerous and attacks it by flooding the body with chemicals, resulting in a range of symptoms. Depending on whether an immunoglobulin (IgE) antibody is involved, allergies are classed as either IgE-mediated or non-IgE-mediated, or in some cases a mixture of the two. This all sounds quite technical, but there is a reason that I have mentioned it.

Although we typically think of allergies invoking a very quick and scary reaction, the reality is that some allergies can actually result in a delayed, milder range of symptoms. For instance, the symptoms of IgE-mediated allergies are more immediate, appearing within minutes, and may include (but are not limited to) sneezing, vomiting, abdominal pain, hives, swelling of the face and/or throat, or pallor. Symptoms of a non-IgE-mediated allergy are generally much slower to appear, potentially taking several hours to days to make themselves known, and may include eczema, diarrhoea, vomiting or constipation.

Although we typically think of allergies as invoking a very quick and scary reaction, the reality is that some allergies can actually result in a delayed, milder range of symptoms.

More severe, life-threatening allergic reactions are known as anaphylaxis, but it is incredibly rare for allergic babies to show such a strong reaction. Indeed, globally there have been no reported cases of any baby under the age of 12 months dying from anaphylactic shock due to food. And although food allergies are on the increase, they still affect the minority of babies and children, and most will grow out of their food allergies over time.

COMMON FOOD ALLERGENS

More than 170 foods are known to have triggered severe allergic reactions. The most common ones are:

- eggs • cow's milk • peanuts • tree nuts such as hazelnuts or cashews • fish • shellfish • wheat • sesame • soya

PROTECTING AGAINST FOOD ALLERGIES

For the past few decades, it was usual practice to delay the introduction of common food allergens to babies. Recent research suggests that this practice has probably done more harm than good. There appears to be an early window of opportunity for introducing food allergens, somewhere around 4–6 months, when a baby's immune system may be trained to accept them. Consequently, it's now recommended that all babies be given allergenic foods such as peanut butter, cooked eggs, and dairy and wheat products in their first year of life, including babies at a high risk of allergy. As a result, I don't particularly shy away from the use of common food allergens in my recipes, especially because they're very tasty and nutritious.

Food intolerances

Food hypersensitivities that don't involve the immune system are more commonly known as food intolerances. As with allergies, there's a wide range of constituents in food that we can be intolerant to – for instance, chemicals called histamines and salicylates that are naturally present in some foods, or additives including monosodium glutamate. Accordingly, it can be very difficult to pinpoint what the

issue is, and it would be impossible to go through all the known culprits and their symptoms here. Instead, I have focused on the most prevalent (although still relatively rare) intolerance, which is lactose intolerance.

LACTOSE INTOLERANCE

Lactose is the sugar found in all mammalian milks, including breast milk, where its relatively high content compared to other milks is thought to support rapid brain growth in infancy. Intolerance to lactose (sometimes called lactose malabsorption) means that there is a lack of or insufficient amounts of the enzyme lactase, which is needed to break it down. Subsequently, undigested lactose passes into the bowel, where bacteria ferment it, producing gases and discomfort, and sometimes diarrhoea or constipation.

In extremely rare cases, called primary lactose intolerance, babies don't produce any of the enzyme lactase needed to digest lactose. Most cases are secondary lactose intolerance, however, which is temporary and happens as a result of damage to the gut lining – where lactase is made. This may materialise after a bout of gastroenteritis, uncontrolled coeliac disease or if the baby is exposed to something to which they are allergic or intolerant (other than lactose).

Provided the gut is given time to heal, secondary lactose intolerance will resolve in time. Depending on the cause, treating it may mean restricting the amount of lactose in the diet, as well as dealing with any other issues that may have triggered the damage. Note that, if you're breastfeeding, reducing dairy in your diet will have no bearing on the lactose content of your milk, and you don't need to stop breastfeeding with lactose intolerance.

Gluten-related hypersensitivities

Gluten is the main protein found in wheat, and this term is generally also used to describe the very similar proteins that are found in barley and rye. A seemingly increasing number of people suspect that they or their children have gluten hypersensitivity, and so cut gluten out of their diets. Given this can be quite restrictive and compromise nutrient intake, I want to outline some important points to consider before you go down this route.

There are three main conditions typically associated with gluten hypersensitivity. The first of these is coeliac disease, a lifelong condition where the body responds to gluten by invoking an immune response that causes damage to the lining of the small intestine. Symptoms may include severe constipation, diarrhoea, weight loss or lack of weight gain, nutrient deficiencies due to poor absorption such as anaemia, bloating, flatulence and irritability. Sometimes there may be no symptoms at all.

The second is wheat allergy, which is an IgE-mediated food allergy that children commonly outgrow by school age. Most wheat-allergic children also suffer from atopic dermatitis, and immediate symptoms following wheat ingestion are similar to those for other food allergens, such as hives and breathing difficulties.

The third is non-coeliac gluten sensitivity, which is less well understood than the first two – both of which need ruling out before a diagnosis can be made. Symptoms may include tummy ache, bloating, change in bowel habits or, more broadly, tiredness, headache, bone and joint pain, eczema or a rash. These signs usually closely follow the consumption of gluten and disappear when gluten is withdrawn.

As you can see, there's quite a lot of overlap between the symptoms for gluten hypersensitivities and, as the degree of dietary restriction needed differs depending on which condition a person has, a proper medical diagnosis is always recommended. Furthermore, unlike with other food hypersensitivities where culprit foods should be eliminated and advice sought, it is important to continue consuming gluten before a diagnosis is made because blood tests look for antibodies that are present only when gluten is around.

. . . .

In the early days you may feel as if all your baby does is eat, sleep, poop and repeat, but the rate of soiled nappies does reduce to an average of one or two a day by their first birthday (thank goodness).

. . . .

A NOTE ON OATS

Oats contain a gluten-like protein called avenin in smaller amounts than are found in the triticale tribe (barley, rye and wheat) and are problematic to advise on because studies that have looked at whether people with coeliac disease react to them have reported mixed results. Oats may also be contaminated with gluten from other grains during processing. People with diagnosed gluten hypersensitivity should seek personalised advice from their gastroenterologist on whether oats are OK. For this reason, I have not labelled oat-containing recipes in this book as gluten-free.

Tummy troubles

In the early days you may feel as if all your baby does is eat, sleep, poop and repeat, but the rate of soiled nappies does fall to an average of one or two a day by their first birthday (thank goodness). Note that breastfed babies tend to pass stools that are softer and generally more frequent than those of formula-fed babes.

A little cherry-red face when your baby passes a bowel motion is completely normal in the early months of weaning. Their bodies are still getting used to solid foods and, even by their first birthday, three-quarters of babies will still have visible bits of food in their nappies, which can be a bit uncomfortable to push out. Indeed, half of 2-year-olds and a third of 3-year-olds may still be popping out visible dinner remnants – this is completely normal.

CONSTIPATION

When we talk about constipation, we are referring to the infrequent passage of small or hard stools, with or without straining. Several things can cause constipation, and it's often seen when weaning commences, as the body adapts to the transition from milk or formula to solids, and again around 2 years of age, when potty training begins. Common causes include dehydration or poor fluid intake, fever and poor diet.

Sometimes passing a large, hard stool can cause a tear in the back passage, known as a fissure, which can sting and be painful on subsequent bowel movements. This can exacerbate the problem of constipation because little ones may be reluctant to go to the toilet when they need to. Fissures are quite common from 6 to 24 months and may cause bleeding.

Before introducing softening laxatives, we would usually check food and fluid intake to see whether this could be adjusted to help ease the discomfort. Stools are a mixture of undigested foods, bacteria from the large bowel, water and intestinal cells. Most of this undigested food is plant material (fibre) or non-digestible carbohydrates. If there are insufficient plant foods in the diet, this could cause constipation and, vice versa, increasing plant foods can help to ease it. Moreover, some plant foods act as prebiotics, and are food for the good bacteria that support healthy bowel habits.

Ripe pears, apples (not raw chunks – see page 26 on choking) and prunes are known to be particularly helpful in relieving constipation, as they contain fructose and sorbitol, sugars that draw fluids into the bowel and soften the stools.

Most plant foods provide fibre, such as whole grains, fruit, vegetables, legumes and nuts (not whole – see page 26 on choking). Using these as a foundation for meals is important. My only caveat to this is unripe bananas, which can sometimes aggravate constipation. As these are a favourite first food, consider easing their consumption and/or make sure that they're soft and ripe. Also avoid giving extra fibre that isn't in wholefood form, such as bran or psyllium husk.

Increasing fibre intake may make constipation worse if fluid intakes are not increased to match. This is because water makes up quite a lot of stools and is important in keeping them soft. It's worth noting here that too much milk can sometimes exacerbate constipation because this can displace fibre-containing foods in the diet (see section on drinks, pages 37–40).

DIARRHOEA

It's very common for little ones to have short bouts of diarrhoea. Generally these are caused by an infection such as gastroenteritis and will usually resolve within 7 days. Diarrhoea is nature's clever way of flushing out harmful bacteria and toxins, but in doing so considerable amounts of fluid can be lost. The main thing we want to prevent here is dehydration – signs of which would include fewer wet nappies, darker urine or sunken eyes.

Oral rehydration solutions (ORSs) are recommended for maintaining hydration during bouts of diarrhoea. It is usually advised that breastfed babies consume these alongside their normal breastfeeds, and formula-fed babies should have ORS instead of formula for 6 hours. You can continue to offer foods, although be mindful that your little one's appetite may drop.

A couple of probiotic strains have been shown to be effective at reducing the duration of infective and antibiotic-induced diarrhoea; these are *Lactobacillus rhamnosus* GG and *Saccharomyces boulardii*. They are available in powdered form for babies and children, or some brands of plain or Greek-style yoghurt may include them – check the label.

Longer lasting (chronic) diarrhoea is generally put down to 'toddler diarrhoea' and appears between the ages of 12 months and 5 years, spontaneously resolving itself after some time. Symptoms of this would include frequent, watery stools with undigested foodstuffs in a child who is otherwise well and thriving. The cause of toddler diarrhoea is somewhat of a mystery, and so doctors would usually rule out other potential causes such as a food intolerance, before settling on this diagnosis.

Spring

Shelling peas, scrubbing new potatoes, tearing leafy herbs, juicing zesty citrus ... Spring brings a growing warmth and cleansing air that lifts nature out of winter's hibernation. A time for nourishing pies to fill hungry tummies, second breakfasts of oaty stewed rhubarb loaf, and melon and cucumber gazpacho to soothe and restore.

Almond Buttermilk Porridge
with Cherry Compote

MAKES 4 ADULT PORTIONS OR 8 BABY PORTIONS

This recipe is best on fresh spring mornings, when the air is crisp and you want something soothing and unfussy. Years of porridge making has taught me that I usually prefer my morning oats cooked in their soaking water, but this recipe instead has a milk base, made creamier by stirring through a generous helping of my vanilla cardamom almond butter. Stirring in nut butter is a good way of adding more nutrition to a milk base, especially with almond milk, where the pulp generally does not make it into the milk itself. Serve the porridge warm with a dollop of the cherry compote and its juices on top.

VANILLA CARDAMOM ALMOND BUTTER

200 g (7 oz/1¼ cups) whole natural almonds, soaked overnight

1 vanilla bean or ½ teaspoon unsweetened vanilla bean powder (ground vanilla; see page 237)

½ teaspoon ground cardamom

PORRIDGE

500 ml (17 fl oz/2 cups) milk

2 tablespoons vanilla cardamom almond butter (see above)

95 g (3¼ oz/1 cup) rolled (porridge) oats (see note on page 104)

CHERRY COMPOTE

150 g (5½ oz/1 cup) cherries, pitted

juice of 1 large orange (remove pips)

To make the almond butter: Rinse and drain the soaked almonds, then dry-toast in a large frying pan for 3–4 minutes over medium heat. Empty into a food processor. Use a small, sharp knife to split the vanilla bean, and scrape the seeds in with the almonds. Add the cardamom and process for 8–10 minutes until smooth.

This recipe makes about 170 ml (5½ fl oz/⅔ cup); it will keep for up to a week if stored in a sealed jar or container with a tight-fitting lid in the refrigerator.

To make the porridge: Whisk together the milk and almond butter in a medium saucepan until thoroughly mixed. Add the oats, cover and leave to soak in the refrigerator overnight.

When ready to cook, bring the oats to a gentle simmer and cook, partially covered, for 10 minutes.

To make the compote: Put the cherries and orange juice in a small saucepan, and simmer, uncovered, for 10 minutes. Remove from the heat, and carefully mash with a fork or use a hand-held blender to purée if you want a smoother consistency.

For little ones: Once cool, this 'poddige', as my older son used to call it, should be tacky enough for babies to self-feed by hand or to stick to a spoon. Stir in the crimson juices well for beginners.

PREPARATION TIME 15 minutes, plus overnight soaking **COOKING TIME** 10 minutes

⫸ DIETARY INFO Dairy-free option (use plant-based milk) • vegetarian • vegan option (use plant-based milk)

Toasted Coconut Bread
with Fermented Berry Salsa

MAKES 4 ADULT PORTIONS OR 8 BABY PORTIONS

Enjoying French bread – or eggy bread, as we used to call it – as a child at Brownie camp is as vivid to me as if it happened yesterday. It's a humble breakfast, easy to make with only a few ingredients and a frying pan. Yet, as a child, it always felt like such a special treat. Fermenting the salsa with whey is optional, but quick to do the night before — and it has the added benefit of topping up good bacteria in the gut and getting the day off to a vibrant start.

FERMENTED BERRY SALSA

75 g (2½ oz/½ cup) strawberries

80 g (2¾ oz/½ cup) blueberries

grated zest and juice of 1 small unwaxed lemon (remove pips)

pinch of unsweetened vanilla bean powder (ground vanilla; see page 237)

1 tablespoon whey (optional; see page 240)

TOASTED COCONUT BREAD

250 ml (9 fl oz/1 cup) coconut cream

4 eggs

1 banana, sliced

½ teaspoon unsweetened vanilla bean powder

90 g (3¼ oz/1 cup) unsweetened desiccated (finely shredded) coconut

coconut oil for frying

8 sourdough bread slices (preferably wholemeal [whole-wheat])

To make the salsa: Whiz all the salsa ingredients in a blender or food processor until you obtain the desired consistency. I prefer a few chunks left in my salsa, but beginners will need it to be smooth.

Pour the salsa into a clean 500 ml (17 fl oz/2 cup) jar, close the lid tightly and leave at room temperature for 12–24 hours to ferment. Store in the refrigerator if not using immediately.

To make the coconut bread: Put the coconut cream, eggs, banana and vanilla bean powder in a blender or food processor, and pulse until smooth. Pour into a wide, shallow dish. Empty the desiccated coconut into another dish of equal size.

Heat 1 teaspoon coconut oil in a large frying pan over medium heat and, as that is coming up to the right temperature, soak a slice of bread in the eggy custard mixture for a few seconds on each side. Transfer to the other dish, and coat with the coconut on both sides.

Carefully place the bread in the pan, and fry for 1–2 minutes on each side, until the egg is cooked and some of the coconut has toasted and turned golden brown. Turn out the cooked bread onto a plate, and repeat until all the slices have been used, adding more coconut oil as needed. Slice into fingers, ready to dip into the salsa.

For little ones: *If your baby has not quite mastered dipping, hand over the bread fingers pre-dipped. Toasted coconut can make quite a lot of crumbs for little ones, so go lightly when coating their toast.*

PREPARATION TIME 10 minutes, plus overnight fermenting **COOKING TIME** 20 minutes

≫ DIETARY INFO Dairy-free option (use plant-based milk) ● nut-free ● vegetarian

Lemon and Chia Pancakes
with Roasted Blueberries

MAKES 10–12 PANCAKES

Day to day, we generally eat a simple warm porridge for breakfast, rotating grains such as oats, buckwheat or quinoa that have been soaked and lightly fermented overnight, and adding flavour with seasonal fruits and toasted nuts and seeds. Breaking from this routine for our 'Saturday-morning pancake' ritual marks the beginning of the weekend – a chance to take a little longer over breakfast and chat about how we're going spend the next two days together as a family.

With an abundance of blueberries on our tables comes the promise of longer, warmer days. In this recipe, I find they need nothing more than a short roast with vanilla to celebrate them. When their tight coats pop open with hot, bubbly juices, they're ready to spoon straight from the baking paper onto these warm, fluffy pancakes.

310 ml (10¾ fl oz/1¼ cups) milk

6 soft medjool dates, pitted

250 g (9 oz/1⅔ cups) blueberries

1 vanilla bean or ½ teaspoon unsweetened vanilla bean powder (ground vanilla; see page 237)

150 g (5½ oz/1 cup) wholemeal (whole-grain) spelt flour

1 teaspoon bicarbonate of soda (baking soda)

grated zest and juice of 1 unwaxed lemon (remove pips)

2 eggs

1 tablespoon coconut oil, melted, plus extra for frying

1 tablespoon chia seeds

Preheat the oven to 190°C (375°F). Line a roasting tin with baking paper.

Make your sweetened milk base by putting the milk and dates in a small saucepan over medium–low heat. Bring to a gentle simmer, and leave to soften and infuse for 10 minutes. Remove from the heat, then carefully whiz with a hand-held blender until smooth. Pour the date milk into a large jug for quicker cooling while you prepare the other ingredients.

Put the blueberries in a bowl. Use a small, sharp knife to split the vanilla bean and scrape the seeds into the blueberries. Stir well, empty into the prepared roasting tin and roast for 15 minutes, until the berries have started to release their juices. Remove from the oven, and carefully lift out the baking paper full of blueberries and juice. Transfer the berries and juice to a bowl, ready for heaping onto the pancakes at the table.

Meanwhile, whisk together the flour, bicarbonate of soda and lemon zest in a large bowl and set aside.

Beat the lemon juice, eggs and the 1 tablespoon coconut oil into the sweetened milk base, then pour into the dry ingredients. Continue beating until the ingredients are just combined. Be careful not to over-mix, or you'll end up with rubbery pancakes. The batter should be bubbly, lumpy and light, rather than smooth and thick. Little pockets of flour are fine, but big streaks where the ingredients have not been mixed enough are not.

Use a large frying pan over medium heat to cook several pancakes at once, allowing 1 teaspoon coconut oil per pancake. Bring the oil up to heat, and once it is hot measure out 2 tablespoons of batter for each pancake (to make bear pancakes, add a little extra batter to make two ears). Sprinkle a pinch of chia seeds on top of each pancake when the batter goes into the pan. Cook until bubbles start to appear in the batter and the pancake easily lifts off the bottom of the pan, then flip over and fry the other side until golden brown.

For little ones: *Cut the cooled pancakes into fingers, and hand them to your baby smeared in the burst blueberry juices.*

PREPARATION TIME 15 minutes **COOKING TIME** 25 minutes

≫ DIETARY INFO Dairy-free option (use plant-based milk) ● nut-free ● vegetarian

Oat and Olive Oil Loaf
with Rhubarb Swirls

MAKES 1 LOAF

For those cooler, sometimes drizzly spring mornings, there's nothing lovelier than a slice of this sweet breakfast loaf with its perky pink swirls. Best enjoyed slightly warm from the oven, try it smothered thickly in vanilla labneh (see page 240). One slice with a steamy cup of fresh tea or coffee is a guaranteed to recharge the batteries of any tired parental soul.

165 g (5¾ oz/1⅓ cups) chopped fresh rhubarb (about 2 stalks)

juice of 1 orange (remove pips)

215 g (7½ oz/1¾ cups) oatmeal (Scottish oats/ground oats; see note on page 104)

25 g (1 oz/¼ cup) rolled (porridge) oats (see note on page 104), plus extra for sprinkling

25 g (1 oz/¼ cup) unsweetened desiccated (finely shredded) coconut

1½ teaspoons aluminium-free baking powder (see page 236)

1 teaspoon unsweetened vanilla bean powder (ground vanilla; see page 237)

4 eggs

125 ml (4 fl oz/½ cup) mild olive oil

125 ml (4 fl oz/½ cup) milk

60 ml (2 fl oz/¼ cup) maple syrup

Preheat the oven to 200°C (400°F). Grease and flour a 19 x 8 cm (7½ x 3¼ inch) loaf tin.

Put the rhubarb, orange juice and 80 ml (2½ fl oz/⅓ cup) water in a saucepan over medium–high heat, and simmer, uncovered, for 10 minutes to soften. Remove from the heat and carefully purée with a hand-held blender until smooth. Set aside.

Whisk together the oatmeal, the rolled oats, desiccated coconut, baking powder and vanilla bean powder in a large bowl. In a large jug, beat together the eggs, olive oil, milk and maple syrup until well combined. Pour the wet ingredients into the dry ingredients, and use a spatula or metal spoon to mix well. Set aside for a couple of minutes to thicken.

Layer the batter and the purée several times in the prepared baking tin, finishing with a layer of batter. Use a knife to gently swirl the two layers around. Sprinkle a small handful of extra rolled oats on top of the loaf. Cover with a piece of baking paper to prevent burning.

Bake for 50 minutes, or until a skewer inserted into the centre of the loaf comes out clean. Remove from the oven, and leave the loaf in the tin until cool enough to handle, then transfer to a wire rack. Serve warm or cold, cut into slices.

For little ones: *Slice into fingers for easy gripping.*

PREPARATION TIME 20 minutes **COOKING TIME** 50 minutes
≫ DIETARY INFO Dairy-free option (use plant-based milk) • nut-free • vegetarian

Spiced Almond Fritters
with Pumpkin and Apple

MAKES 10

I try to instil a rhythm and a gentle routine into the days with my children, as I think it is important to help them feel calm, secure and grounded. Enjoying a nourishing breakfast together is such an important part of that, bringing us together, waking our minds and bodies, and providing fuel for the morning's exploration and endeavours.

This fritter recipe can be easily adapted by using other seasonal fruit and sweet vegetables such as firm pears in place of the apple, or carrots, sweet potatoes or parsnips instead of squash. You may just need to adjust the cooking times slightly.

4 eggs

250 g (9 oz/2 cups) peeled and grated butternut pumpkin (squash)

3 eating apples, cored

3 tablespoons almond meal

½ teaspoon ground cinnamon

½ teaspoon ground ginger

¼ teaspoon ground cardamom

coconut oil for frying

maple syrup (optional), to serve

To make the batter, beat the eggs well in a large bowl. Add the pumpkin and grate in one of the apples, along with the almond meal and spices. Stir to combine. Finely slice the remaining 2 apples and set aside.

Working in batches and allowing 1 teaspoon coconut oil per fritter, heat the coconut oil in a large frying pan over medium heat. Once the oil is hot, spoon 2 tablespoons of the fritter batter into the pan, and shape into a fritter using a spoon or spatula. Continue until you have three or four fritters in the pan, taking care not to overcrowd the pan. Press a slice of apple into the top of each fritter. Cook for 3–4 minutes on the first side, then flip over and cook for a further 1–2 minutes until cooked through and crisp and golden on the outside. Keep warm on a plate lined with paper towel while cooking the rest. Repeat until all the batter has been used. Serve the fritters drizzled with a little maple syrup, if you like.

For little ones: *As raw apple presents a choking hazard for babies, these fritters are a great way to introduce this fruit in its whole form. The apple slice is unlikely to be soft enough for beginners, so either leave this off their fritter or grate all the apples into the batter. You may need to add a little more almond meal if the apples are especially juicy.*

PREPARATION TIME 10 minutes **COOKING TIME** 15 minutes

DIETARY INFO Dairy-free • gluten-free • vegetarian

Beef and Black Bean Tostadas
with Spelt Tortillas and Tomatoes

MAKES 4 ADULT PORTIONS OR 8 BABY PORTIONS

These tostadas use tortilla bases for a lighter pizza-style dinner. I have topped them with slow-cooked, pull-apart beef, but you can use whatever toppings you prefer. You could also speed this dish up immensely by leaving out the beef and simply cooking the beans and sauce through, or by choosing a quicker cut of meat and frying it off on the stovetop.

I have given my recipe here for soaked tortilla wraps. Soaking flour in this way makes the mineral nutrients in the wholemeal flour more available and also has the added benefit of making the tortillas softer. I would usually soak these the night before – or in the morning if it's the weekend. If you do not have time to do this or have not thought ahead to soak the flour among the morning chaos, you can of course speed up the preparation by opting for carefully selected ready-made tortillas.

SPELT TORTILLAS

250 g (9 oz) wholemeal (whole-grain) spelt flour

100 g (3½ oz/⅔ cup) unbleached white spelt flour

125 ml (4 fl oz/½ cup) coconut oil, plus extra for frying

2 tablespoons linseeds (flaxseeds)

1 tablespoon good-quality apple cider vinegar

185 ml (6 fl oz/¾ cup) warm filtered water

coconut oil for frying (optional)

To make the tortillas: Whiz together the flours, coconut oil, linseeds and vinegar in a food processor until all the oil has been absorbed. Transfer to a large bowl, and add the warm water. Bring together into a ball with your hands, and turn out and knead on a clean work surface for 10 minutes until soft and greasy. Alternatively, transfer to an electric stand mixer with a dough hook, and let that do all the work for you. Cover the dough with plastic wrap, and leave at room temperature for 12–24 hours to ferment.

Divide the dough into four pieces, shape each one into a ball, then flatten into circles with your hands to make four tortilla shapes. Using a rolling pin, roll out as thinly as you can without breaking.

Heat a large, dry frying pan over medium–high heat, and when hot add one of the tortillas. Dry-fry for 2–3 minutes on the first side, then flip and dry-fry the other side for a further 1–2 minutes. There should be no 'wet' flour left, and the tortilla should be cooked through. Transfer to a plate and cover with a damp tea towel (dish towel); repeat with the other three tortillas.

You can either use the tortillas soft or fry them for a second time to firm them up. Bring about 2 teaspoons of coconut oil to a medium heat in the same frying pan or on a flat griddle, and fry for 1–2 minutes on each side. Transfer to a plate, ready to serve.

BEEF AND BLACK BEAN FILLING

1 tablespoon olive oil

500–600 g (1 lb 2 oz – 1 lb 5 oz) whole piece of beef (choose a lean cut suitable for slow-cooking, such as chuck or braising steak)

1 red onion, finely chopped

500 g (1 lb 2 oz) tomatoes, quartered

1 red capsicum (pepper), seeds and membrane removed, roughly chopped

4 garlic cloves, finely chopped

¼ teaspoon chilli flakes

200 g (7 oz/1 cup) cooked and drained black beans

salad and sour cream or labneh (see page 240), to serve

To make the filling: Preheat the oven to 170°C (325°F).

Put the oil in a roasting tin over medium heat on the stovetop. Add the beef and onion, and seal the meat for 3–4 minutes on each side.

Meanwhile, whiz the tomatoes, capsicum, garlic and chilli flakes in a blender food processor until you have a pulpy sauce. Add to the roasting tin, and stir through the beans. Cover and roast for 3–4 hours, or until the meat pulls apart easily with two forks.

To assemble: Smear sour cream onto each tortilla, top with a portion of the tomato beef and beans, and add any salad vegetables you like. Serve warm.

For little ones: *Keep the tortilla soft rather than frying for a second time to firm up, and finely chop any salad leaves if you're giving to a toothless beginner. You may find it easier to mash the beans and layer the filling between two tortillas or one folded in half, and then cut into finger-shaped strips for easy gripping.*

PREPARATION TIME 30 minutes, plus 12–24 hours' fermenting **COOKING TIME** 3–4 hours

➤➤➤ DIETARY INFO Dairy-free option (omit sour cream/labneh) ● gluten-free option (use gluten-free wraps) ● nut-free

Fish and Spring Veg Parcels
with Zesty Coconut Dressing

MAKES 4 ADULT PORTIONS OR 8 BABY PORTIONS

For children and grown-ups alike, there's something a bit special about being given a little present to unwrap at dinnertime. Granted, little ones may not fully appreciate the delight in soft, flaky fish at such a tender young age and wonder why you aren't bestowing upon them a colourful new toy. Still, cooking fish like this, tightly wrapped in a paper parcel to catch all the steam, is one of the best ways to keep it moist and flavourful. You can, of course, use any seasonal vegetables here, as long as the size of the pieces will allow for quick cooking because the fish doesn't take long.

80 ml (2½ fl oz/⅓ cup) coconut oil, melted, plus extra, to coat baking paper

5 kaffir lime leaves, stems removed

1 handful coriander (cilantro) leaves

2 tablespoons unsweetened desiccated (finely shredded) coconut

1 x 2 cm (¾ inch) piece of root ginger, peeled

4 sustainably caught skinless and boneless white fish fillets (about 500 g/1 lb 2 oz)

8 baby (Dutch) carrots, halved lengthways and parboiled for 3–4 minutes

1 zucchini (courgette), halved lengthways and cut into julienne

125 g (4½ oz/¾ cup) cherry tomatoes

boiled new potatoes, to serve

Preheat the oven to 200°C (400°F). Prepare the baking paper by cutting four squares measuring 40 cm (16 inches) along each side. Fold each square in two, then draw half a (vertical) heart shape from the crease. Cut along the line, and open out to form a full heart shape.

To make the dressing, pulse the coconut oil, kaffir lime leaves, coriander, desiccated coconut and ginger in a blender or food processor until thick.

On one half of each piece of baking paper, layer the fish, a drizzle of dressing, a quarter of the vegetables and a little more dressing before closing. Seal by folding over the other half of the baking paper and, beginning at one edge, work around to carefully and tightly fold the two sides together. Gently transfer to a baking tray and brush with the extra coconut oil. Bake for 15 minutes until the fish has just cooked through. Serve with boiled new potatoes. Once unwrapped, check the fish for any little bones, just to be safe.

For little ones: *In this recipe, I recommend parboiling the carrots first because they're unlikely to be soft enough for beginners when cooked straight from fresh in this way. Allow enough time for the meal to cool before handling. There may be a lot of steam when the fish is unwrapped, so even older toddlers may need a hand with opening.*

PREPARATION TIME 15 minutes **COOKING TIME** 15–25 minutes (if parboiling carrots)
⫸ DIETARY INFO Dairy-free ● gluten-free ● nut-free

Lentil and Root Vegetable Pies
with a Spelt Pastry Crust

MAKES 8 INDIVIDUAL PIES

For those sunny spring days when you can't help but get out of the house and into the fresh air to explore, I pack these pocket-sized parcels of nourishment to take with us for eating cold later.

Pies have a bit of a bad reputation for being cheap, stodgy and unhealthy, but that needn't be the case. Here, I have used a wholesome olive-oil-based crust that you can repurpose to cover a pot pie. Alternatively, use it to make a sweet version filled with seasonal fruits, adding spices such as cinnamon or vanilla in place of the nutritional yeast.

OLIVE OIL PASTRY

220 g (7¾ oz/1½ cups) wholemeal (whole-grain) spelt flour

150 g (5½ oz/1 cup) unbleached white spelt flour

125 ml (4 fl oz/½ cup) olive oil

1 tablespoon nutritional yeast (optional; see page 237)

2 eggs, beaten separately (1 in pastry, 1 for brushing)

Preheat the oven to 200°C (400°F). Line a large baking tray with baking paper.

To make the pastry: Whiz together the flours, oil and nutritional yeast in a food processor until you have a fine, crumbly texture. Transfer to a large bowl, then add 100 ml (3½ fl oz) cold water and one of the beaten eggs, and mix in with a fork until absorbed. Bring the pastry together into a ball with your hands, then remove from the bowl and knead for 5 minutes on a clean work surface. Cover the pastry with a slightly damp tea towel (dish towel), and chill in the refrigerator for 15 minutes.

To make the filling: Put the oil in a medium frying pan over medium–low heat. Add the onion and sauté for 5 minutes until soft. In a small bowl, mix together the cornflour and 1 tablespoon cold water until smooth, then add to the onion with the stock, carrot and parsnip. Simmer over a medium–low heat for 8–10 minutes until

LENTIL AND ROOT VEGETABLE FILLING

1 tablespoon olive oil

1 small onion, finely chopped

1 tablespoon cornflour (cornstarch)

125 ml (4 fl oz/½ cup) vegetable stock

1 small carrot (leave unpeeled), finely chopped

1 small parsnip, finely chopped

100 g (3½ oz/2 cups) cooked brown lentils, well drained

1 tablespoon fresh thyme leaves

cooked and thickened. Transfer to a deep bowl or jug, and purée using a hand-held blender. Stir through the lentils and thyme, and set aside.

To assemble: Split the pastry in half. Roll out one half into a rectangle on a large, clean chopping board until the pastry is 3 mm (⅛ inch) thick. Cut into eight smaller rectangles about 8 x 10 cm (3¼ x 4 inches). Spoon filling onto each of the rectangles, leaving a little space at the edge of each one to seal. Roll out the second half of the pastry in the same way, making the lids slightly bigger than the bases, and either prick with a fork or make a shape with a pastry cutter. Place on top of the filling, then use a fork to press down the edges to seal. Transfer to the prepared baking tray, brush with the remaining beaten egg, and bake for 30 minutes until golden brown and cooked through.

For little ones: *Once cool enough to handle, slice the pies into halves or quarters so that your baby has easy access to the juicy filling.*

PREPARATION TIME 30 minutes **COOKING TIME** 30 minutes

≫ DIETARY INFO Dairy-free ● nut-free ● vegetarian

Red Capsicum Pasta Bake
with Tomatoes and Harissa

MAKES 4–6 ADULT PORTIONS OR 8–12 BABY PORTIONS

This recipe is one to have up your sleeve when the house looks like a bomb went off and you have laundry coming out of your ears. The thick sauce is made by quickly whizzing up the ingredients in the food processor. You then pour it over the pasta and, an hour later, a hearty tray bake arrives on the table, straight from the oven, ready to satisfy even the hungriest of tummies.

620 g (1 lb 6 oz/4 cups) chopped red capsicums (peppers)

400 g (14 oz) fresh tomatoes, roughly chopped

40 g (1½ oz/¼ cup) sun-dried tomatoes

50 g (1¾ oz/½ cup) almond meal

2 soft medjool dates, pitted

4 garlic cloves

2 tablespoons olive oil

½ teaspoon harissa paste

420 ml (14½ fl oz/1⅔ cups) milk

250 g (9 oz/2¾ cups) wholemeal (whole-wheat) fusilli pasta

Preheat the oven to 200°C (400°F).

Whiz together all the ingredients except the milk and pasta in a food processor until smooth. Pour into a large ceramic baking dish, add the milk and pasta, and stir well. Make sure that you tuck in any pasta under the sauce so that the tips don't burn.

Cover with a layer of baking paper, and bake for 60 minutes until bubbling and piping hot. Carefully remove from the oven and stir well before serving.

For little ones: *You can scoop out your baby's portion 10–15 minutes before the rest of the pasta has finished cooking, and spread it out on a dish for quicker cooling.*

PREPARATION TIME 10 minutes **COOKING TIME** 1 hour
DIETARY INFO Dairy-free option (use plant-based milk) • vegetarian • vegan option (use plant-based milk)

Roast Veg and Chickpea Burgers
with Chilli and White Miso

MAKES 8 BURGERS

Proving burgers can be epically healthy, this wholesome recipe contains a simple mix of flavourful roast vegetables, chickpeas for plant protein and sesame seeds for healthy fats. You'd be hard-pushed to squeeze any more nutrients into a humble bread roll. And don't freak at the mention of the word chilli; it's purely to provide a little warmth. Try this topped with salad and a nutritious spread such as Pea and Macadamia Nut Pesto (see page 92) or Roast Beetroot Hummus (page 200).

300 g (10½ oz/5 cups) broccoli florets

1 carrot, roughly chopped

1 small red onion, roughly chopped

2 tablespoons olive oil

¼–½ teaspoon chilli flakes

200 g (7 oz/1 cup) cooked chickpeas, rinsed and drained

60 g (2 oz) quinoa flakes

1 egg

½ teaspoon white miso paste (see page 237)

80 ml (2½ fl oz/⅓ cup) hot water

40 g (1½ oz/¼ cup) sesame seeds

salad and wholemeal (whole-grain) sourdough bread rolls, to serve

Preheat the oven to 220°C (425°F).

Spread out the broccoli, carrot and red onion on a baking tray, drizzle over the olive oil and sprinkle over the chilli flakes. Roast for 20 minutes, then remove the tray from the oven and turn the temperature down to 200°C (400°F).

Transfer the roast vegetables to a food processor, and add the chickpeas, quinoa flakes and egg. Set aside.

Mix together the miso paste and hot water in a cup until the miso has dissolved, and carefully pour onto the baking tray to pick up any of the leftover roasting juices. Decant the miso stock into the food processor, and blend until combined. The mixture will be wet but not sticky.

Line the baking tray with baking paper.

Make balls of the burger mix using a couple of tablespoons for each one, then gently roll in the sesame seeds to coat. Press down and shape into patties on the prepared baking tray. Return to the oven and bake for 15 minutes to cook through and firm up.

For little ones: *Adjust the amount of chilli you include, maybe starting with a pinch and working your way up from there. Cut these burgers in half or quarters for easier gripping.*

PREPARATION TIME 15 minutes **COOKING TIME** 35 minutes
>>> DIETARY INFO Dairy-free • gluten-free option (use gluten-free bread) • nut-free • vegetarian

Bean and Minted Pea Fishcakes
with a Golden Quinoa Crust

MAKES 12 FISHCAKES

White bean mash is a great alternative to mashed potato in dishes such as these fishcakes or potato-topped pies. Beans are digested and absorbed more slowly than mashed potato and so are easier for the body to deal with. They also add a boost of plant protein, making any fish or meat go further.

Another trick I've used here is to use quinoa flakes in place of breadcrumbs, reducing the salt content of the dish and again adding another hit of plant protein. Serve these with a crunchy spring salad, if you like.

250 g (9 oz) sustainably caught skinless and boneless fish fillet

juice of ½ lemon (remove pips), plus 1 extra, cut into wedges and pips removed, to serve

2 tablespoons olive oil, plus extra for frying

400 g (14 oz/2 cups) cooked and drained cannellini beans

125 ml (4 fl oz/½ cup) milk

50 g (1¾ oz/½ cup) grated cheddar cheese

180 g (6 oz) quinoa flakes

½ teaspoon ground mustard seeds

155 g (5½ oz/1 cup) fresh or thawed frozen peas

2 tablespoons finely chopped fresh mint

75 g (2½ oz/½ cup) plain (all-purpose) flour

2 eggs, beaten

Preheat the grill (broiler) to medium–high. Line a baking tray with baking paper. Place the fish on the prepared baking tray and drizzle over the lemon juice and half the olive oil. Season with freshly ground black pepper. Grill for about 6 minutes, or until cooked through.

Meanwhile, purée the beans and milk in a blender or food processor until smooth. Transfer to a small saucepan, and add the cheese, half the quinoa flakes, the ground mustard seeds and the remaining olive oil. Gently heat and stir until all the cheese has melted. Set aside.

Flake the fish into a large bowl, removing any stray little bones. Add the bean mash and stir through the peas and mint. Use your hands to scoop out the fishcake mixture and make palm-sized balls. Dip in the flour, egg and then the remaining quinoa flakes. Place on a plate until ready to cook. I find it easiest to prepare six fishcakes at a time and make the next batch while those first six are cooking. I set a timer so that I don't forget to turn over the ones in the pan.

Bring 2 tablespoons of extra oil to medium heat in a large frying pan, place the fishcakes in the pan and gently flatten with a spatula or tongs. Fry for 3–4 minutes until golden underneath, then flip over and repeat. Transfer to a plate and repeat with the second batch. Serve warm, with the lemon wedges for squeezing over.

For little ones: *Cut the fishcakes in half for easier gripping.*

PREPARATION TIME 15 minutes **COOKING TIME** 20 minutes

>>> DIETARY INFO Gluten-free option (use gluten-free flour) • nut-free

Refried Bean Burritos
with Scrambled Tofu

MAKES 4 ADULT PORTIONS OR 8 BABY PORTIONS

Meals such as this go down really well in our house and are on regular rotation. These burritos can be eaten at any time of the day, hot or cold; are easily adapted to suit most dietary needs, be it gluten-free or vegan; and make it easy to swap in seasonal produce. If you've never had scrambled tofu, live on the edge and please trust me when I say you that won't miss the egg.

Allowing children to serve themselves at the table and to have a hand in the making of their meal is also a great way of giving them some control, particularly in terms of how much food goes onto their plate. Children are naturally very good masters of their own appetite, a skill that we often lose as adults. There's also lots of fun to be had, rolling up wraps and precariously holding them so that the filling doesn't spill out and the juices dribble down our wrists.

SCRAMBLED TOFU

300 g (10½ oz) silken tofu

1 tablespoon olive oil

1 carrot, grated

1 tablespoon finely chopped sun-dried tomatoes

80 g (2¾ oz/½ cup) finely chopped green capsicum (pepper)

4 garlic cloves, finely chopped

¼ teaspoon sweet paprika

¼ teaspoon ground turmeric

REFRIED BEANS

1 tablespoon olive oil

1 red onion, finely chopped

2 garlic cloves, finely chopped

¼ teaspoon ground cumin

¼ teaspoon smoked paprika

To make the scrambled tofu: Press the tofu to remove some water by sandwiching it between several sheets of paper towel and two plates. (I usually pop on a weight such as a heavy teapot or saucepan, to help things along.) Leave to stand for 5–10 minutes; the paper towel should be damp.

Heat the olive oil in a large frying pan over medium heat. Add the pressed tofu and the remaining scrambled tofu ingredients, and fry for 10 minutes, stirring regularly. Empty into a serving bowl when ready. The tofu should crumble when heated and stirred, to make a scrambled egg texture.

To make the refried beans: In a second frying pan, heat the olive oil over medium heat. Add the onion, garlic, cumin and paprika, and fry for 5 minutes to soften. Add the beans and 60 ml (2 fl oz/¼ cup) water, and fry for a further 10 minutes, stirring regularly to prevent burning. Add the coriander, and cook for a further 2 minutes. Lastly, add the milk, mash and empty the refried beans into a serving bowl.

200 g (7 oz/1 cup) cooked and drained mixed beans

1 large handful finely chopped coriander (cilantro)

1 tablespoon milk

TO SERVE

4–8 wholemeal (whole-wheat) wraps (or use wholemeal [whole-grain] spelt and flaxseed tortillas from the tostada recipe, see page 72)

sour cream or labneh (optional; see page 240)

grated cheese such as cheddar (optional)

salad leaves (optional)

To assemble: Spread each wrap with some scrambled tofu and refried beans, along with any other fillings you choose to use, such as sour cream, grated cheese or lettuce leaves. Roll up tightly.

For little ones: *The easiest way to prepare these is to spread the filling on one side of the wrap, fold it in half, then cut it into fingers for easy gripping. The refried beans will also stick well to a spoon for self-feeding.*

PREPARATION TIME 20 minutes **COOKING TIME** 20 minutes

⋙- DIETARY INFO Dairy-free option (use plant-based milk and omit sour cream/labneh and cheese to serve) ● gluten-free option (use gluten-free wraps) ● nut-free ● vegetarian ● vegan option (as for dairy-free option)

Baked Beef Meatballs
with Beetroot and Quinoa

MAKES ABOUT 20 MEATBALLS

These sweet, earthy meatballs are a simple, wholesome alternative to shop-bought, processed meat products, which are often full of cheap fillers, preservatives and added salt. Thanks to the beetroot juices, they're delicious enough to be enjoyed with the addition of only some chunky pasta. But if you fancy a quick sauce as well, I often just whiz up a can of plum tomatoes or four or five fresh tomatoes, with a sprinkle of dried oregano, and heat this through.

500 g (1 lb 2 oz) beetroot (beets) (about 3)

½ whole garlic bulb, top trimmed off

3 tablespoons olive oil

500 g (1 lb 2 oz) lean beef mince (ground beef)

1 red onion, finely chopped

40 g (1½ oz/¼ cup) sun-dried tomatoes

70 g (2½ oz) quinoa flakes

1 egg, beaten

2 teaspoons dried oregano

cooked chunky wholemeal (whole-wheat) pasta such as penne rigate, to serve

Preheat the oven to 220°C (425°F).

Trim both ends of the beetroot, then chop the flesh into cubes (there's no need to peel the beetroot). Empty onto a baking tray with the garlic, and lightly drizzle with 2 tablespoons of the olive oil. Roast for 20 minutes. Remove the tray from the oven and set aside. Reduce the oven temperature to 200°C (400°F).

Meanwhile, fry the mince and red onion in the remaining 1 tablespoon olive oil in a large frying pan over medium heat for 10 minutes until browned and softened. Transfer to a food processor, and add the sun-dried tomatoes, cooked beetroot and roast garlic slipped from its skins. Pulse briefly until there are no large chunks of beetroot remaining. Empty into a large bowl and stir through the quinoa flakes, egg and oregano. Season with freshly ground black pepper.

Line a baking tray with baking paper or grease with a little olive oil. Shape the meat mixture into balls, space out evenly on the prepared tray and bake for 10 minutes. Serve with the pasta of your choice.

For little ones: *These soft meatballs are not as messy as you would think. The quinoa flakes soak up most of the beetroot juice, and your baby shouldn't end up bright pink in the process of enjoying them (more's the pity). Cut them in half for easier gripping.*

PREPARATION TIME 15 minutes **COOKING TIME** 30 minutes
DIETARY INFO Dairy-free ● gluten-free option (use gluten-free pasta) ● nut-free

Chunky Minestrone
with Giant Croutons

MAKES 6–8 ADULT PORTIONS OR 12–16 BABY PORTIONS

This soup is made for those early spring days when you just want to hunker down and are craving a comforting cup of soup to warm you through. In this version of minestrone, I've used borlotti beans in the base and kept the vegetables really chunky and substantial. Add any extra seasonal vegetables you have to hand.

MINESTRONE

1 brown onion, finely chopped

6 garlic cloves, finely chopped

1 celery stalk, thickly sliced

2 tablespoons olive oil

200 g (7 oz/1 cup) tinned borlotti beans, rinsed and drained

40 g (1½ oz/¼ cup) sun-dried tomatoes

1.5 litres (52 fl oz/6 cups) chicken stock

2 carrots, roughly chopped

400 g (14 oz) tomatoes, quartered

3 tablespoons chopped fresh oregano

2 zucchini (courgettes), sliced into 2.5 cm (1 inch) chunks

90 g (3¼ oz/1 cup) wholemeal (whole-wheat) pasta such as fusilli

CROUTONS

250 g (9 oz) crusty whole-grain sourdough bread

35 g (1¼ oz/⅓ cup) finely grated parmesan cheese

1 teaspoon dried oregano

2 tablespoons olive oil

To make the soup: In a large saucepan, warm the olive oil over medium heat. Add the onion, garlic and celery, and fry gently for 10 minutes to soften.

Meanwhile, purée the beans, sun-dried tomatoes and 80 ml (2½ fl oz/⅓ cup) of the stock until smooth. Add to the pan with the remaining stock, as well as the carrots, tomatoes and oregano. Bring to the boil, then reduce the heat and simmer, uncovered, for 20 minutes. Add the zucchini and pasta, and simmer for a further 10 minutes or until cooked al dente. Serve the soup hot, topped with the crunchy croutons.

To make the croutons: Preheat the oven to 200°C (400°F). Cut the bread into large chunks and put in a bowl. Add the parmesan cheese, oregano and olive oil, and stir well to coat. Spoon and press any of the remaining cheesy topping that may have settled to the bottom of the bowl onto the bread as you transfer it to a baking tray. Spread out and toast in the oven for 15 minutes.

For little ones: *I've designed this soup with little ones in mind, so the vegetables are large enough to hold once cool and the beans are blended into the base for slurping from a cup (with help if needed). Croutons can be quite crunchy for beginners, so keep some to one side without toasting, or soften with a little of the soup base.*

PREPARATION TIME 20 minutes **COOKING TIME** 30 minutes

≫– DIETARY INFO Dairy-free option (omit parmesan cheese) ● gluten-free option (use gluten-free bread and pasta) ● nut-free ● vegetarian option (use vegetable stock)

Melon and Cucumber Gazpacho
with Coconut Milk Kefir

MAKES 4 ADULT PORTIONS OR 8 BABY PORTIONS

This cool, pulpy soup is made for those sunny spring days when the first ripe strawberries come into season and you want something light. I'd suggest that it's more of a starter (appetiser) or snack than a meal on its own, but it's also perfect if you or your little one has been off food with a tummy bug or sickness. The melon, cucumber and coconut flavours are gentle and soothing, and the coconut milk kefir is full of restorative probiotics.

Kefir is simple to make at home, and we regularly use it in place of standard milks in uncooked dishes (cooking will kill the probiotics) such as for soaking muesli or in smoothies or ice popsicles. You can use different plant or animal-based kefir milks in this recipe – or standard milks will work just as well, although without the extra good bugs (see page 241 for more information).

80 g (2¾ oz/½ cup) pepitas (pumpkin seeds), soaked for at least 8 hours beforehand, plus extra, to serve

250 ml (9 fl oz/1 cup) coconut milk kefir (see page 241), chilled

1 rockmelon (about 1 kg/2 lb 4 oz), peeled, seeded and diced

1 cucumber, peeled, seeded and sliced

150 g (5½ oz/1 cup) strawberries, sliced

Rinse and drain the soaked pepita seeds, then dry-toast them in a small frying pan over medium heat for 3–4 minutes, tossing gently to prevent burning. They may just start to crackle as you remove them from the heat. Empty into a blender or food processor, and blend until you have a fine seed meal. Add the coconut milk kefir, melon and cucumber, and whiz until pulpy.

Serve with the sliced strawberries and extra pepitas.

For little ones: Be mindful to make the topping age-appropriate. For babies, finely chop or grind the pepita sprinkle, and keep the strawberries whole or offer them 'cutted up', as my son used to say, to be used as dippers.

PREPARATION TIME 10 minutes, plus 8 hours' soaking **COOKING TIME** 4 minutes

DIETARY INFO Dairy-free • gluten-free • nut-free • vegetarian • vegan

Pea and Macadamia
Nut Pesto

MAKES ABOUT 500 ML (18 FL OZ/2 CUPS)

This creamy pea pesto is a bright spring staple that we keep in the refrigerator to use throughout the week for spreading on toast, dolloping into soups or stirring through pasta for a quick but nutrient-packed meal. You can swap the macadamias for other nuts such as cashews or almonds, or try pepitas (pumpkin seeds) if you need a nut-free version.

235 g (8½ oz/1½ cups) fresh or thawed frozen peas

125 ml (4 fl oz/½ cup) extra virgin olive oil

75 g (2½ oz/½ cup) macadamia nuts

40 g (1½ oz/scant ½ cup) finely grated parmesan cheese

1 large handful basil leaves

juice of 1 lemon (remove pips)

1 garlic clove

Put all the ingredients in a food processor, season with freshly ground black pepper and pulse until combined. Alternatively, pound the ingredients into a paste using a mortar and pestle. If not using the pesto immediately, transfer to a suitable container, cover in a layer of olive oil, seal tightly and pop into the refrigerator until needed; it will keep for up to 5 days if stored this way.

For little ones: *Try this stirred through chunky spiral pasta or on toast with a sprinkle of cheese.*

PREPARATION TIME 5 minutes
DIETARY INFO Gluten-free • vegetarian

Grilled Paneer Dip
with Broad Beans and Mint

MAKES ABOUT 500 ML (17 FL OZ/2 CUPS)

I have fond memories of shelling broad beans at my grandma's house as a child, and I love bringing home a big paper bag of them to entertain Laurence for a bit.

Paneer is an excellent cheese for little ones because it's simply the pressed curds from milk, without any added salt. It has a similar texture to haloumi, or 'squeaky cheese', as Laurence and I always jokingly call it. Paneer doesn't melt when cooked, and so grilled and served as it is here it makes for a warm, chunky spread.

200 g (7 oz) paneer cheese

2 garlic cloves

1 tablespoon olive oil

310 g (11 oz) fresh or thawed frozen broad beans (about 1¾ cups fresh; 2 cups frozen)

60 ml (2 fl oz/¼ cup) extra virgin olive oil

juice of ½ lemon (remove pips)

1 large handful mint leaves

Preheat the grill (broiler) until hot. Line a baking tray with baking paper.

Place the block of paneer on the baking paper with the whole garlic cloves. Drizzle with the olive oil, and season with some freshly ground black pepper. Grill for 10 minutes, or until starting to brown.

Meanwhile, steam the broad beans for 3–5 minutes until softened.

Reserve a quarter of the grilled paneer, and put the remainder in a blender or food processor. Carefully peel and add the garlic cloves, then the cooked broad beans, extra virgin olive oil, lemon juice and mint. Blend or process for about a minute. The dip should be lumpy and thick. Serve sprinkled with the reserved paneer.

For little ones: *Spread this onto some chunky whole-grain sourdough toast fingers, or try as a dip for baked potato chips (fries).*

PREPARATION TIME 10 minutes **COOKING TIME** 10 minutes

≫ DIETARY INFO Gluten-free ● nut-free ● vegetarian

Mango and Orange Popsicles
with Carrot and Ginger

MAKES 10 x 90 ML (3 FL OZ) POPSICLES

If you ever want an honest critique of your cooking, there is nothing more telling than the verdict of baby's facial expression. There's a wonderful sense of anticipation when you give a baby a food to try for the first time, especially something bright and zingy such as these icy bursts of flavour. As a parent you can but sit there, waiting for that split second to pass as their minds compute what they're doing, before revealing their opinion so brilliantly across their face.

Thanks to the antioxidant pigment beta-carotene, these luminous ice popsicles are such a vibrant orange colour that you almost feel as if you are slurping in the sun's energy directly.

315 g (11 oz/1 cup) roughly diced frozen mango

1 orange, peeled and segmented (remove pips)

1 large carrot, roughly chopped

1 x 5 cm (2 inch) piece of fresh root ginger, peeled

Put all the ingredients in a blender or food processor, add 250 ml (9 fl oz/1 cup) water and whiz until smooth. Pour into the popsicle (ice-block/ice lolly) moulds, dividing the mixture evenly. Transfer to the freezer, and leave for at least 4 hours until firm.

For little ones: *Popsicles are not just cooling on warmer days; they're ideal to soothe and numb sore, achy gums during teething as well. Look for smaller moulds that will be more manageable for little hands.*

PREPARATION TIME 10 minutes **FREEZING TIME** at least 4 hours
≫ DIETARY INFO Dairy-free ● gluten-free ● nut-free ● vegetarian ● vegan

Lemon Curd Tart
with Maple Syrup and Vanilla

MAKES 6–8 ADULT PORTIONS OR 12–16 BABY PORTIONS

The first food I ever gave to Laurence was a lemon. I was zesting it and could tell from his wildly waving hands that he wanted a closer look. Of course, his reaction to tasting it was one I will not forget and, for that reason, a lemon tart was a must for this book. You can omit the agar-agar and the curd will still be reasonably firm enough to slice, especially after chilling. It does work better with a setting agent, though, if you can source it. If not using agar-agar, simply skip the cooking step and transfer the curd straight into the tart base after blending.

FILLING

1 teaspoon agar-agar powder (see notes)

grated zest and juice of 2 unwaxed lemons (remove pips), plus 1 extra

155 g (5½ oz/1 cup) unsalted raw cashews (see notes)

300 g (10½ oz) silken tofu

2 tablespoons maple syrup

1 tablespoon coconut oil

¼ teaspoon unsweetened vanilla bean powder (ground vanilla)

TART BASE

80 g (2¾ oz/½ cup) whole natural almonds (see notes)

115 g (4 oz/¾ cup) pepitas (pumpkin seeds; see notes)

90 g (3¼ oz/1 cup) unsweetened desiccated (finely shredded) coconut

125 ml (4 fl oz/½ cup) coconut oil, melted

15 soft medjool dates, pitted

½ teaspoon ground ginger

Line an 18 cm (7 inch) loose-based flan (tart) tin with baking paper.

To make the filling, in a small bowl, dissolve the agar-agar in the lemon juice, then set aside. Blend or process the cashews until creamy. Add the remaining filling ingredients, including the agar-agar mixture, and continue to process until smooth.

Transfer the curd to a medium saucepan, and gently simmer over low heat for 5 minutes. Remove from the heat and set aside.

Next, make the tart base. Pulse all the ingredients in a clean food processor for about 20 seconds until a sticky crumble forms. Use your fingers to press the crumble into the prepared tin, starting with the bottom, then making the sides.

Pour the filling into the tart base, and chill in the refrigerator for at least 1 hour. Cut the extra lemon into thin slices and remove any pips. Arrange the lemon slices on top of the tart and serve.

For little ones: *Slice into fingers for easy gripping, and have your camera at the ready.*

Notes: *Agar-agar, a gelatine substitute and thickener, is a flavourless seaweed product suitable for vegetarians and vegans. A stronger setting agent than gelatine, it should be used sparingly.*

This tart is even gentler on little stomachs – and more nutritious – if the following three ingredients can be soaked, rinsed and drained before using: cashews, 2 hours; almonds, 8 hours; pepitas, 8 hours.

PREPARATION TIME 15 minutes, plus 2–8 hours' soaking (optional) **COOKING TIME** 5 minutes **CHILLING TIME** 1 hour
➽ DIETARY INFO Dairy-free ● egg-free ● gluten-free ● vegetarian ● vegan

Summer

Charring peaches, bursting berries, softening sweet leeks, slow-cooking lamb ... Summer fills our cups with blue skies and balmy heat, inviting us to lie down in the long grass and watch the clouds wisp by. Tossing salads with vibrant green dressings and stashing creamy labneh cups in the freezer signal that summer is here.

Buttermilk Waffles
with Carob and Raspberries

MAKES ABOUT 6 WAFFLES

Sometimes, perhaps after a tough week, you need a special breakfast to start the weekend afresh. These waffles are just that. They feel especially indulgent, almost like a dessert, yet they're full of good things. There's sweetness coming from the raspberries and dates, and a malty cocoa flavour from the carob and mesquite.

Mesquite flour can sometimes be a little tricky to get hold of so, if you can't find it at your local health food shop or specialist wholefood grocer, simply replace it with an equal quantity of wholemeal (whole-grain) spelt flour. Using frozen raspberries instead of fresh is also fine, but just be sure to thaw them thoroughly because a soggy waffle makes for a miserable start to the day.

250 g (9 oz/2 cups) fresh or thawed frozen raspberries

230 ml (7¾ fl oz/scant 1 cup) buttermilk

150 g (5½ oz/1 cup) wholemeal (whole-grain) spelt flour

1 tablespoon carob flour (see page 235)

2 teaspoons mesquite flour (optional; see page 236)

1 teaspoon bicarbonate of soda (baking soda)

2 eggs

6 soft medjool dates, pitted

2 tablespoons coconut oil, melted, plus extra for brushing

coconut milk powder, to dust (optional)

Put half the raspberries in a blender or food processor. Add the buttermilk, flours, eggs, dates and the 2 tablespoons melted coconut oil. Blend or process until thick and smooth. Stir through another quarter of the raspberries (half of what's left), reserving the remainder for serving.

Heat up the waffle machine or waffle griddle, brush with a little extra coconut oil and pour over sufficient batter to make a waffle. Cook on a medium setting for 4–5 minutes until the steam stops.

Serve with a dusting of coconut milk powder, if you like, and the reserved raspberries scattered over.

For little ones: *Cut into fingers for easy gripping, and ensure that they've cooled down sufficiently, particularly the pockets of whole raspberry, which can get quite hot.*

PREPARATION TIME 10 minutes **COOKING TIME** 15 minutes
≫ DIETARY INFO Nut-free ● vegetarian

Silverbeet Chickpea Crepes
with Basil and Ricotta

MAKES 10–12 CREPES

It can be quite a challenge to find ways of introducing the flavour and texture of leaves to little ones, as leaves are hard to chew when you don't have teeth or indeed the skills to grind them up. Unearthing more ways to include leaves in their diet should make babies more receptive to them as their taste preferences develop.

Of course, except for their bright green colour, these crepes are almost unrecognisable as leaves, but the flavour is still there. Speaking of which, I'm not going to lie to you. The batter smells of cut grass – and not in the nice reminds-you-of-warm-weekends kind of way, but more in an I'm-not-sure-I-want-to-eat-lawn sort of fashion. Anyway, I promise that this all disappears when they're cooked, and instead you're left with a sweet pancake, perfect for the height of summer.

olive oil for frying

CREPE BATTER
120 g (4¼ oz/1 cup) besan (chickpea) flour

4 eggs

125 ml (4 fl oz/½ cup) vegetable stock

300 g (10½ oz) silverbeet (Swiss chard) (about 3 stalks), stalks removed, roughly chopped

grated zest and juice of 1 unwaxed lemon (remove pips)

1 handful fresh basil leaves

TO SERVE
230 g (8 oz/1 cup) ricotta cheese

100 g (3½ oz/⅔ cup) pine nuts, crushed

extra virgin olive oil, to drizzle

lemon wedges (remove pips)

To make the crepes, put all the batter ingredients in a blender or food processor, and whiz until smooth. You may find little bits of uncut silverbeet remain, which is fine.

Allowing 1 teaspoon of olive oil per crepe, heat the oil in a large frying pan over medium–high heat. Spoon in 2 tablespoons of batter per crepe. (I usually do two or three at a time for speed.) Tilt the pan or use a spoon to gently coax the batter into a circle. Cook for about 3 minutes on the first side, until bubbles begin to appear and the crepe lifts off easily. Flip over and heat for another minute.

Spread the ricotta over the crepes, and sprinkle over the pine nuts and a drizzle of extra virgin olive oil. Season with freshly ground black pepper for the grown-ups, and serve with lemon wedges for squeezing over.

For little ones: *Cut into fingers for easy gripping, and hand over already smothered in the ricotta and crushed pine nuts.*

PREPARATION TIME 10 minutes **COOKING TIME** 20 minutes
➤➤ DIETARY INFO Dairy-free option (omit the ricotta cheese) ● gluten-free ● nut-free ● vegetarian

Sticky Date and Carob Muesli
soaked in Banana Milkshake

MAKES 4 ADULT PORTIONS OR 8 BABY PORTIONS

Since becoming a mother, I've developed a number of simple rules that I like to follow, in the hope of keeping myself from losing the plot entirely. One of these – and perhaps the most important – is about being kind to my future self. What I mean by this is that, if there's something I can do today that the future me will really appreciate, then I'll always try to do it. This might mean laying out clothes the night before, doing a batch-cook on a Sunday so I have an easy weeknight dinner option, or readying a breakfast such as this one the night before, so that I don't have to think about it in my tired, pre-coffee morning haze.

MUESLI

75 g (2½ oz/½ cup) macadamia nuts

95 g (3¼ oz/1 cup) rolled (porridge) oats (see note)

30 g (1 oz/½ cup) flaked coconut

20 g (¾ oz) quinoa flakes

8 soft medjool dates, pitted

2 teaspoons carob flour (see page 235)

BANANA MILKSHAKE

500 ml (17 fl oz/2 cups) milk

2 bananas

2 tablespoons cashew butter

Using a blender or food processor, whiz the macadamia nuts into small pieces but not quite a nut meal, before adding the remaining muesli ingredients and whizzing to a crumble texture. Set aside.

Use a food processor or hand-held blender to purée the milkshake ingredients until smooth. Decant half the milkshake into a large bowl, and stir in the muesli. Cover and refrigerate overnight. Transfer the remaining milkshake into a jug, cover and also refrigerate overnight.

To serve, spoon the soaked muesli into bowls, and top with remaining milkshake as desired.

For little ones: *Add just a smidgen, if any, extra milkshake after soaking to keep the muesli tacky enough to handle or stick to a spoon.*

Note: *Choose unstabilised oats if possible. These haven't been steamed to deactivate their natural enzymes. This does mean that the oats will go rancid more quickly, but the enzymes will help to break down the phytic acid (see page 220) when they are soaked.*

PREPARATION TIME 15 minutes, plus overnight soaking

»» DIETARY INFO Dairy-free option (use plant-based milk) ● vegetarian ● vegan option (use plant-based milk)

Creamy Chia Pudding Cups
with Peaches and Dried Apricots

MAKES 12 CUPS

Creamy chia puddings are one of my favourite ways to enjoy this tiny superseed, but I wanted to think of an easy way babies that could enjoy them without too much risk of the pudding being spattered all over the walls. Here, I've made simple little raw tart cups to hold the puddings – which, after overnight chilling, firm up considerably.

250 ml (9 fl oz/1 cup) milk

3 fresh peaches, halved and stones removed

6 teaspoons chia seeds

130 g (4½ oz/⅔ cup) preservative-free dried apricots

65 g (2¼ oz/⅓ cup) raw buckwheat groats (see note), soaked for at least 1 hour beforehand, then drained

125 g (4½ oz/1¼ cups) almond meal

45 g (1½ oz/½ cup) unsweetened desiccated (finely shredded) coconut

6 soft medjool dates, pitted

2 tablespoons coconut oil

Blend or process the milk, peaches and chia seeds, and allow to stand and thicken for 10 minutes. Stir again or briefly pulse in the blender or food processor, and set aside.

Pulse the dried apricots, buckwheat groats, almond meal, desiccated coconut, dates and coconut oil in a food processor until you have a sticky crumble texture. Spoon about 2 tablespoons of this mixture into each hole of a 12-hole tartlet tin. Press the crumble around the bottom and edges of each hole to make a cup.

Pour in the peachy chia pudding mixture until level with the top edge of each case. Refrigerate overnight before serving.

For little ones: *Slice the cups in half to make for easier gripping.*

Note: *Buckwheat groats are the hulled seeds of buckwheat. The seeds' tough outer layer is removed, and the seeds are then crushed into smaller pieces, known as 'groats'. You can buy buckwheat groats that have already been toasted, but it is definitely the untoasted ones you want here.*

PREPARATION TIME 15 minutes, plus 1 hour's soaking and chilling overnight
➤➤ DIETARY INFO Dairy-free option (use plant-based milk) ● gluten-free ● vegetarian ● vegan option (use plant-based milk)

Dutch Baby Pancake Bowl
with Roast Plums and Labneh

MAKES 4 ADULT PORTIONS OR 8 BABY PORTIONS

This is such a beautiful-looking dish it could almost double as a dessert if you wanted it to. I love the alchemy of a Dutch baby pancake – how it puffs up in the oven, without the need for any leaveners such as yeast or baking powder. Once removed, it quickly releases its air, creating a natural bowl for any nourishing ingredients you have to hand. I like to fill this with creamy vanilla labneh and ripe summer stone fruit. The plums take just as long to cook as the pancake, meaning that everything can go fuss-free into the oven together.

PANCAKE BATTER

170 ml (5½ fl oz/⅔ cup) milk

1 tablespoon maple syrup

70 g (2½ oz/½ cup) wholemeal (whole-grain) spelt flour

2 tablespoons mesquite flour (see page 236)

3 eggs

1 teaspoon ground cinnamon

TOPPINGS

3–4 plums, halved and stones removed

1 tablespoon coconut oil, melted, plus 1 extra teaspoon for frying

30 g (1 oz/¼ cup) shelled pistachio nut kernels, to serve

VANILLA LABNEH

180 g (6 oz/¾ cup) labneh (see page 240)

pinch of unsweetened vanilla bean powder (ground vanilla; see page 237)

In a medium bowl, whisk together all the batter ingredients until smooth. Cover and chill for at least 20 minutes (an hour is better).

Preheat the oven to 220°C (425°F). Place a 23 cm (9 in) ovenproof frying pan or ceramic pie dish in the oven, and line a baking tray with baking paper. Brush the plums with the 1 tablespoon melted coconut oil, and arrange cut side up on the baking tray. Set aside.

Carefully remove the hot frying pan from the oven. Add the extra 1 teaspoon coconut oil and, when this has melted, pour in the batter. Place the frying pan at the bottom of the oven and the baking tray in the middle, and cook for 20 minutes.

Meanwhile, put the labneh in a small bowl. Add the vanilla bean powder and whip into the labneh using a whisk or spoon. Whiz the pistachios to your preferred texture using a food processor or hand-held blender, or roughly crush using a mortar and pestle.

While the pancake is still warm, heap on the vanilla labneh, followed by the plums, then sprinkle over the crushed pistachios. Cut into the desired portions, and serve immediately.

For little ones: *Process the nuts into a fine meal, and slice the plums. I haven't found it necessary to peel plums — babies seem to know intuitively how to gum out the side with the sweet fruit — but by all means peel if you feel it's necessary.*

PREPARATION TIME 10 minutes, plus 20–60 minutes' chilling **COOKING TIME** 20 minutes

⋙ DIETARY INFO Nut-free option (omit pistachio nut kernels) ● vegetarian

Charred Zucchini and Peaches
with Almond Quinoa

MAKES 4 ADULT PORTIONS AS A STARTER OR SIDE DISH OR 8 BABY PORTIONS

Charring produce on the barbecue is one of the signs that summer has well and truly arrived. Of course we get to crank up the barbecue a little more in Australia than when we lived in the United Kingdom, but the novelty of cooking al fresco is not wasted on us. Barbecuing or chargrilling is also a good way to cook and soften produce for little ones. It is quick, albeit at a high temperature, and does not need water. This means the nutrient loss is somewhat limited.

Peaches and zucchini cooked this way are perfectly soft and juicy, and also easy for little ones to hold. Simple to put together, with few ingredients, this dish can serve as a light meal on a balmy day, a starter or a side dish.

100 g (3½ oz/½ cup) tricolour quinoa

250 ml (9 fl oz/1 cup) almond milk

80 ml (2½ fl oz/⅓ cup) balsamic vinegar

4 zucchini (courgettes), halved lengthways

2 white peaches, halved and stones removed

olive oil for grilling

Rinse the quinoa well until all the soapy bubbles disappear. Transfer to a medium saucepan and add the almond milk. Bring to the boil, then reduce the heat to a simmer, cover and leave to cook for 15 minutes until all the milk has been absorbed. Remove from the heat and set aside.

Meanwhile, pour the balsamic vinegar into a small saucepan over medium heat, and gently simmer, uncovered, until reduced to a thick syrup, about 10 minutes. Remove from the heat and set aside.

Preheat the barbecue (grill) or a chargrill pan until hot. Scoop out the seeds from the zucchini with a metal spoon and discard (into the compost heap, if you have one). Brush the zucchini and peaches with olive oil, and grill on the barbecue or in the chargrill pan for 3–4 minutes until softened and charred.

Spoon the cooked quinoa into the zucchini boats. Slice the peaches, if you like, and arrange on top. Drizzle with the balsamic reduction, and serve warm.

For little ones: *Push the quinoa firmly into the boat, and cut the zucchini into fingers for easy gripping. I generally don't bother peeling either the zucchini or the peach for a baby to gum out the fleshy inside. The skin also gives them something firm to hold on to.*

PREPARATION TIME 10 minutes **COOKING TIME** 20 minutes
≫ DIETARY INFO Dairy-free ● gluten-free ● vegetarian ● vegan

Lemony Buckwheat Risotto
with Green Peas and Leek

MAKES 4 ADULT PORTIONS OR 8 BABY PORTIONS

This risotto, or 'buckotto' (a name I guess may be more apt), uses some of my favourite sweet summer flavours, including leeks, lemon and peas. Cooked for long enough and with plenty of nourishing stock or broth, buckwheat makes a wonderful creamy, nutty base to which you can add any seasonal vegetables.

Although buckwheat masquerades as a grain, it's not related to wheat at all. Rather surprisingly, rhubarb would be its closest relative. Buckwheat also stands out because, along with soya beans, hempseeds, amaranth and quinoa, it's one of the few plant foods that contain all the essential amino acids. This makes it a fabulous staple to keep on hand for a plant-based diet.

1 tablespoon olive oil

1 leek, finely chopped

2 garlic cloves, finely chopped

195 g (6¾ oz/1 cup) raw buckwheat groats (see note on page 105)

750 ml (26 fl oz/3 cups) vegetable stock

juice of ½ lemon (remove pips)

390 g (13¾ oz/2½ cups) fresh or thawed frozen peas

250 ml (9 fl oz/1 cup) milk

finely grated parmesan cheese, to serve

Heat the olive oil in a large frying pan over medium–low heat. Add the leek and garlic, and allow to sweat for 5 minutes to soften slightly. Next, add the buckwheat and heat for another minute, tossing gently. Pour in the stock and lemon juice, bring to a simmer, cover and cook for 15 minutes.

Meanwhile, using a blender or food processor, purée half the peas with the milk until smooth. Add to the risotto along with the remaining whole peas for the last 5 minutes of the cooking time. Be sure not to overcook this risotto, or it will turn a dull green.

Serve with a sprinkle of finely grated parmesan.

For little ones: *As the risotto cools, it will become tacky and an interesting texture for babies to scoop up directly – or it should stick well to a spoon. Blend all peas for beginners, but cooked whole peas are fine when your little one has mastered the pincer grip (at around 9 months).*

PREPARATION TIME 10 minutes **COOKING TIME** 20 minutes
⋙ DIETARY INFO Dairy-free option (use plant-based milk and omit the parmesan cheese) ● gluten-free ● nut-free ● vegetarian ● vegan option (use plant-based milk and omit the parmesan cheese)

Heirloom Tomato Frittata
with Onions and Mustard Seeds

MAKES 4 ADULT PORTIONS OR 8 BABY PORTIONS

Frittata is a staple dish in our kitchen. Load it with any seasonal produce and herbs you have to hand, whack it under the grill (broiler) and you have a wholesome meal in less than 30 minutes. We would serve this with heaps of shoots, leaves and buttery boiled potatoes. Yum.

1 tablespoon olive oil

5 spring onions (scallions), finely chopped

½ teaspoon mustard seeds

8 eggs

125 ml (4 fl oz/½ cup) milk

150 g (5½ oz) heirloom tomatoes, halved or quartered, depending on size (about ½ cup)

Preheat the grill (broiler) to high.

Heat the oil in an ovenproof frying pan over medium-high heat. Add the spring onions and mustard seeds, and sauté for 5–6 minutes until softened. Whisk together the eggs and milk in a bowl or jug, then pour into the frying pan. Gently stir the egg mixture to spread out the spring onion and seeds. Space the tomatoes, cut side up, evenly around the frittata. Continue to cook for 5 minutes until the edge of the frittata starts to pull away from the side the pan.

Move the pan to under the grill, and cook for a further 5–7 minutes until golden brown on top and just cooked through.

For little ones: *For real beginners, it's a good idea to roughly chop a few of the tomatoes and make a section of the frittata just for your baby – chopped tomato should be easier to deal with than half a small tomato. Alternatively, make a section with just the spring onion and serve quartered medium-sized tomatoes on the side.*

PREPARATION TIME 10 minutes **COOKING TIME** 20 minutes
⋙ DIETARY INFO Dairy-free option (use plant-based milk) ● gluten-free ● nut-free ● vegetarian

Summer Vegetable Soup
with Sweet Potato and Mint

MAKES 6–8 ADULT PORTIONS OR 12–16 BABY PORTIONS

We really try to protect mealtimes at home to ensure that we can fully appreciate and savour our food. For little ones, mealtimes are essential for establishing a good relationship with food, not to mention developing language and conversation skills, and so on. Rushed meals or those where we're distracted make it hard to tune in, truly enjoy the food and listen to our body's signals telling us when we've had enough.

That said, life can get in the way of this. There are often times when we're tending to other things or we might simply be too tired to cook. For those moments, I always like to have several meals in the freezer that I can reheat, confident in the knowledge that they're full of healthy ingredients. This vegetable soup makes a big batch and freezes well for quick midweek meals.

1 tablespoon olive oil

2 celery stalks, sliced

5 spring onions (scallions), sliced

2 garlic cloves, roughly chopped

1 onion, chopped

500 g (1 lb 2 oz/3½ cups) peeled and diced orange-red sweet potato

1 carrot, sliced

1 litre (35 fl oz/4 cups) vegetable stock

125 ml (4 fl oz/½ cup) milk

500 g (1 lb 2 oz/3¼ cups) fresh or frozen peas

1 large handful mint leaves, chopped

Heat the oil in a large frying pan over medium heat. Add the celery, spring onions, garlic and onion. Cook for 10 minutes, stirring occasionally, until the onion has softened.

Add the sweet potato and carrot, and pour in the stock and milk. Bring to the boil, reduce the heat to low, cover and simmer for 10 minutes.

Next, add the peas and mint, cover once again and simmer for a further 5 minutes. (The peas are added at this point so that they are not overcooked.)

Remove from the heat, and use a hand-held blender to process the soup until it has a thick, creamy consistency.

For little ones: *Ensure that the soup is cool enough for your baby. They could try sipping it from a cup (with support), or you could dip toast 'soldiers' (fingers) into it and hand those over.*

PREPARATION TIME 15 minutes **COOKING TIME** 25 minutes

⋙ DIETARY INFO Dairy-free option (use plant-based milk) ● gluten-free ● nut-free ● vegetarian ● vegan option (use plant-based milk)

Chicken with Herby Couscous, Blueberries and Toasted Almonds

MAKES 4 ADULT PORTIONS OR 8 BABY PORTIONS

Whenever I make couscous, I always wonder why I don't make it more often. It must go down as one of the easiest things to prepare – more stress-free than getting the timing right on a boiled egg. For that reason alone, a good-quality wholegrain version should be a staple in the pantry of any busy parent.

Pesto and dressings can be a good way of introducing greenery into the diets of little ones who lack the teeth to tear leaves yet. In this dish the colour, flavour and nutrients from the herby leaves are not lost when added to the beautiful couscous.

40 g (1½ oz/¼ cup) whole natural almonds

60 ml (2 fl oz/¼ cup) olive oil

500–600 g (1 lb 2 oz – 1 lb 5 oz) organic free-range skinless chicken breast fillets

240 g (8½ oz/1¼ cups) whole-wheat couscous

310 ml (10¾ fl oz/1¼ cups) vegetable or chicken stock

250 g (9 oz/1⅔ cups) fresh blueberries, a quarter of them halved

HERB VINAIGRETTE

60 g (2¼ oz/1¾ cups) wild rocket (arugula)

1 handful coriander (cilantro) leaves

80 ml (2½ fl oz/⅓ cup) extra virgin olive oil

juice of 1 lemon (remove pips)

juice of 1 orange (remove pips)

Toast the almonds for 3–4 minutes in a large, dry frying pan over medium–low heat, then set aside to cool.

In the same frying pan, heat the olive oil over medium heat. Add the chicken and sauté for 10–15 minutes until cooked through. Remove from the heat. Shred using two forks to pull the meat apart.

Meanwhile, to make the vinaigrette, whiz together the rocket, coriander, extra virgin olive oil and citrus juices in a blender or food processor until smooth, then set aside.

Tip the couscous into a large bowl or jug, pour over the stock and leave to stand for 5 minutes, until all the stock has been absorbed and the couscous can be fluffed up with a fork.

Halve a quarter of the blueberries, and transfer the couscous, shredded chicken and all the blueberries to a large serving dish. Chop and add the toasted almonds, then stir through the herby vinaigrette, ready to serve.

For little ones: *Chop up the almonds very well or use a food processor to make a fine crumb for sprinkling, and mash into the couscous along with the blueberries. Once your baby has mastered the pincer grip (usually around 9 months), try offering all the blueberries halved.*

PREPARATION TIME 15 minutes **COOKING TIME** 20 minutes
⋙ DIETARY INFO Dairy-free ● nut-free option (omit the almonds)

Slow-cooked Aromatic Lamb
and Farro with Silverbeet

MAKES 6 ADULT PORTIONS OR 12 BABY PORTIONS

Farro was made for slow dishes. As a whole grain, it takes its time to cook and likes to soak up most of the juices from the tender lamb. Yet the heaped, buttery wilted greens are no sideshow, especially those as colourful and healthful as silverbeet (even more so if you use rainbow silverbeet). This honest meal is one meant for cooler summer days, perhaps just as the leaves are starting to fade and autumn is creeping in. It is a firm favourite for Sunday lunch in our home.

875 ml (30 fl oz/3½ cups) vegetable stock

200 g (7 oz/1 cup) whole farro (see note)

1 onion, finely chopped

800 g (1 lb 12 oz) lamb shoulder

1 tablespoon olive oil

4 garlic cloves, finely chopped

2 teaspoons cumin seeds

1 teaspoon ground coriander

500 g (1 lb 2 oz) silverbeet (Swiss chard) (about 4 stalks), stalks and leaves roughly chopped

1 tablespoon unsalted butter (preferably grass-fed)

Preheat the oven to 170°C (325°F).

Put the stock, farro and onion in a large ceramic roasting dish. Place the lamb on top, then brush with the olive oil. Rub the garlic, cumin and coriander into the top of the lamb. Cover the dish, and carefully transfer to the oven. Cook for 4 hours.

Remove the lamb from the oven, and gently pull the meat apart using two forks; mix through the farro. Set aside to rest.

In a large frying pan over medium heat, fry the silverbeet stalks in the butter for 5 minutes until starting to soften. Add the leaves and cook for a further 4–5 minutes until slightly wilted. Stir through the lamb and farro, and you're ready to serve.

For little ones: *Even when cooked, silverbeet stalks will probably be too crunchy for toothless little ones. You may need to chop up the leaves quite well and mash some of the farro into the gravy.*

Note: *Farro has a characteristic nutty flavour and chewy texture. The term refers to three ancient hulled wheat species still grown in Italy today: farro piccolo (einkorn), farro medio (emmer) and farro grande (spelt, or dinkel). All three are sold dried in their whole-grain form, retaining their bran and nutrients. Pearled farro (farro perlato) has had some of its bran removed, so it cooks more quickly and does not need soaking first. Farro medio (emmer) is the type most usually available. Look for farro in good supermarkets, delicatessens, specialty grocers and wholefood outlets.*

PREPARATION TIME 15 minutes **COOKING TIME** 4 hours, plus 10 minutes
⟫⟫ DIETARY INFO Dairy-free ● nut-free

Fish Curry with Coconut,
Coriander and Lemon Naan

MAKES 4 ADULT PORTIONS OR 8 BABY PORTIONS

Just a touch of madras curry powder and cumin give a gentle warmth to this soothing, creamy curry, and seasonal greens such as leeks, zucchinis and peas provide sweetness. As the fish doesn't need long to cook, this dish is fairly quick to pull together. It's really just a matter of giving the naan dough time to rest and soften. You can skip or shorten that step, but you'll get a much denser result. Alternatively, serve with coconut chapattis (see page 188), which are quicker to make, or your favourite grain.

LEMON NAAN

150 g (5½ oz/1 cup) wholemeal (whole-grain) spelt flour

150 g (5½ oz/1 cup) unbleached white spelt flour

2 teaspoons aluminium-free baking powder (see page 236)

grated zest and juice of 1 unwaxed lemon (remove pips)

60 ml (2 fl oz/¼ cup) plain yoghurt

1 tablespoon coconut oil, melted, plus extra, to coat the dough

125 ml (4 fl oz/½ cup) warm water

15 g (½ oz/¼ cup) flaked coconut

2 tablespoons roughly chopped coriander (cilantro)

To make the naan: Whisk together the flours, baking powder and lemon zest, in a large bowl until well combined. Add the yoghurt and the 1 tablespoon coconut oil, and mix with a spoon or your hands to get a crumble texture. Pour in the warm water, and bring the dough together with your hands. Knead for at least 10 minutes either by hand on a clean work surface or using an electric standard mixer with a dough hook attached, until you get a soft, spongy dough. Shape into a ball, then lightly coat in a layer of extra coconut oil before resting (this prevents it drying out). Cover and leave to rest in a warm spot for 1 hour, or until doubled in size.

Preheat the grill (broiler) when ready to cook.

Divide the dough into four equal-sized pieces, and roll out to a 5–6 mm (¼ inch) thickness on a clean work surface. Heat an ovenproof frying pan until very hot. Wet one side of a naan with a little water, and gently place this side down in the hot frying pan. While it's cooking, carefully press some of the flaked coconut and coriander onto the top. Wait until bubbles start to appear – 1–2 minutes – then place the pan under the grill for a further minute or two, to finish cooking and toast the coconut. Remove from the grill and repeat for the other dough pieces. Serve with a drizzle of the lemon juice.

FISH CURRY

1 tablespoon olive or coconut oil

1 leek, finely sliced

1 teaspoon madras curry powder

1 teaspoon cumin seeds

4 sustainably caught skinless and boneless fish fillets (about 500 g/ 1 lb 2 oz)

300 g (10½ oz) zucchini (courgettes) (about 3), finely sliced lengthways into ribbons

400 ml (14 fl oz) coconut milk

35 g (1¼ oz/⅓ cup) almond meal

115 g (4 oz/¾ cup) fresh or frozen peas

To make the curry: Using a large, wide-based saucepan, heat the oil over medium heat. Add the leek, and sauté for 5–6 minutes until softened. Add the curry powder and cumin seeds, and stir well to coat the leeks in the fragrant spices. Add the fish and zucchini, cover and cook for 10 minutes. Finally, add the coconut milk, almond meal and peas, and cook, uncovered, for a further 5 minutes. Serve hot.

For little ones: *Keep some larger chunks of fish to one side, and carefully check them for any little bones. Slice some of the zucchini (courgettes) into fingers instead of ribbons for easier gripping.*

PREPARATION TIME 20 minutes, plus 1 hour for resting the dough **COOKING TIME** 30 minutes

>>> DIETARY INFO Dairy-free option (use coconut yoghurt)

Paneer and Burghul Salad
with Strawberries

MAKES 4 ADULT PORTIONS OR 8 BABY PORTIONS

This abundant whole-grain salad is perfect for making ahead and taking on a picnic on the warmest of summer days. Play around with the strawberries and cucumber. You can make them ample and chunky – important if you're feeding this to little ones – or small and confetti-like.

175 g (6 oz/1 cup) coarse burghul (bulgur), well rinsed and drained

250 g (9 oz/1⅔ cups) strawberries

2 Lebanese cucumbers

200 g (7 oz) paneer cheese

80 g (2¾ oz/½ cup) pine nuts

MINT VINAIGRETTE

1 handful fresh mint leaves

125 ml (4 fl oz/½ cup) extra virgin olive oil

2 tablespoons good-quality apple cider vinegar (preferably organic, with the 'mother' if possible; see note)

juice of 1 lemon (remove pips)

Put the burghul in a medium saucepan, and add 500 ml (17 fl oz/ 2 cups) water. Bring to the boil, reduce the heat to low and simmer for 20–25 minutes until all the liquid has been absorbed.

Meanwhile, chop the strawberries and cucumbers to the desired size, and pop in a large bowl. Crumble in the paneer and add the cooked burghul and pine nuts.

To make the vinaigrette, whisk together all the ingredients until well combined. Drizzle over the salad and toss through. Season with a little freshly ground black pepper, and serve.

For little ones: *Be sure to crush the pine nuts into the paneer cheese and burghul. This dish is quite sticky, so it should be a fun challenge for babies to scoop it up or alternatively stick it to a spoon. Cut the strawberries and cucumber to a suitable size for easy handling.*

Note: *Apple cider vinegar – also known as cider vinegar, or ACV – is made from fermented apples (cider) or apple must. It is available in organic and unpasteurised forms; these will often contain the 'mother', or mother of vinegar. The mother can cause the vinegar to look cloudy and almost as if it has cobwebs in it. It is added during the fermentation process to turn the alcohol liquid into acetic acid (vinegar). There is no need to be concerned; in fact, some people prefer to use vinegar with the mother, particularly apple cider vinegar. You can even strain it out and use it to make your own, should you be so inclined.*

PREPARATION TIME 15 minutes **COOKING TIME** 25 minutes

⋙ DIETARY INFO Vegetarian ● nut-free

Roast Pumpkin and Ricotta Rotolo
in a Fresh Herb Stock

MAKES 4 ADULT PORTIONS OR 8 BABY PORTIONS

In a similar style to cannelloni, rotolo tubes are made with fresh sheets of lasagna. There's something very therapeutic about the repetitive rhythm of rolling and arranging all the tubes, so this is a great recipe if you need to escape into your mind for a little bit.

In this dish the pasta is bathed in a freshly made summery stock, but you could also try a tomato or cream-based sauce as an alternative.

STOCK

2 tablespoons olive oil

5 French shallots, roughly chopped

3 carrots, finely chopped

2 leeks, sliced

1 large handful basil leaves, plus extra, to serve

1 handful fresh oregano leaves

ROTOLO

600 g (1 lb 5 oz) peeled and seeded butternut pumpkin (squash), cut into 1 cm (½ inch) cubes (about 4 cups)

¼ teaspoon chilli flakes

1 tablespoon olive oil

115 g (4 oz/½ cup) ricotta cheese

2 garlic cloves, crushed

500 g (1 lb 2 oz) fresh lasagna sheets (16 sheets)

fresh basil, to serve

Preheat the oven to 220°C (425°F), and line a baking tray with baking paper.

To make the stock: Heat the olive oil in a large saucepan, add the shallots, carrots and leeks, and sweat over medium heat for 10 minutes, stirring regularly. Add the fresh herbs and 500 ml (17 fl oz/2 cups) water. Cover and leave over low heat while you prepare the rotolo. There's no set time for preparing a stock from scratch. Generally speaking, the longer you steep the vegetables and herbs, the more flavour they'll impart.

To make the rotolo: Spread out the pumpkin on the prepared baking tray. Mix the chilli flakes and olive oil together in a small jug, then drizzle over the pumpkin, ensuring that all the pieces are coated. Roast for 20 minutes until softened, remove from the oven and reduce the oven temperature to 200°C (400°F).

Put the pumpkin in a large bowl, add the ricotta and garlic, and mash together with a fork or potato masher until the mixture is well combined and no large chunks remain.

Cut each lasagna sheet in half crossways, and spread the squash filling on each half, leaving a small gap at either end of each piece, as some of the filling will get pushed out. Roll the prepared lasagna pieces into tubes, then arrange the tubes so they are standing on their ends in a deep ceramic ovenproof dish.

To finish: Remove the stock from the heat, and strain out the vegetables and herbs through a sieve set over a bowl. Transfer the stock to a jug, and carefully pour over the pasta, making sure that the rotolo tubes are covered with stock. Cover and bake for 15 minutes.

Serve in a bowl with a little of the stock and some fresh basil scattered on top.

For little ones: *The stock can be hot, so drain the pasta before serving. A rotolo is perfect for babies to hold and squeeze out the filling, which incidentally is light enough not to stain if it goes everywhere – which it will, I have no doubt.*

PREPARATION TIME 20 minutes **COOKING TIME** 35 minutes
»»» DIETARY INFO Nut-free ● vegetarian

Fragrant Chicken Broth
with Broccoli and Noodles

MAKES 4 ADULT PORTIONS OR 8 BABY PORTIONS

Little ones delight in dribbling delicious broth down their chins and slurping up the noodles. Broths are very quick to bring together using whatever simple provisions you have. Seasonal vegetables are easily substituted and tofu can be used in place of meat. Use a little miso paste (see page 237) if you're rushed, and also try using coconut water in place of stock for extra sweetness and nourishment. The kuzu, which is entirely optional, adds a glossy thickness to the broth.

1 tablespoon coconut oil

2 large organic free-range skinless chicken breast fillets (about 500 g/1 lb 2 oz), sliced

5 spring onions (scallions), finely chopped

½ mild green chilli, seeded and finely chopped

2 garlic cloves, crushed

1 x 2 cm (¾ inch) piece of fresh root ginger), peeled and crushed

2 litres (70 fl oz/8 cups) chicken stock or 1 litre (35 fl oz/4 cups) chicken stock and 1 litre (35 fl oz/ 4 cups) unsweetened coconut water

½ lemongrass stem, woody end bashed with a rolling pin

360 g (12¾ oz/6 cups) broccoli florets

2 tablespoons kuzu, crushed (optional; see note)

180 g (6 oz) wholemeal (whole-wheat) ramen noodles

1 large handful coriander (cilantro) leaves, roughly chopped

Melt the coconut oil in a large, wide-based saucepan or wok, and fry the chicken breast, spring onion, chilli, garlic and ginger for 5 minutes until the chicken is white on all sides and the spring onions have softened.

Add the stock, lemongrass and broccoli, bring to the boil and simmer for 5 minutes.

Meanwhile, dissolve the kuzu, if using, in 60 ml (2 fl oz/¼ cup) cold water, then pour into the pan. Add the noodles and coriander, and simmer for a further 5 minutes.

Remove the lemongrass stem before serving.

For little ones: *Strain the liquid for quicker cooling of the broccoli, chicken and noodles. Finely chop the coriander if you're serving to a toothless one. Depending on their ability, you could get them to slurp the broth from a cup, or support the spoon as they bring this to their mouth.*

Note: *Kuzu (or kudzu) is a Japanese root used in its powdered form as a thickening agent for many dishes. It's gluten-free and lacks the starchy taste of other thickening agents.*

PREPARATION TIME 15 minutes **COOKING TIME** 20 minutes
≫ DIETARY INFO Dairy-free ● gluten-free option (use gluten-free noodles) ● nut-free

Roast Red Capsicum and Cashew Pâté

MAKES ABOUT 250 ML (9 FL OZ/1 CUP)

This plant-based pâté pulls together with just a few ingredients and makes a delicious base for sandwiches and wraps, or simply spread on crackers. If not using immediately or in the unlikely event that you have leftovers, cover with a thin layer of olive oil in an airtight container, seal tightly and refrigerate for up to 3 days.

1 large red capsicum (pepper), seeded and roughly chopped

2 tomatoes, halved

1 tablespoon olive oil

160 g (5¾ oz/1 cup) unsalted raw cashews, preferably soaked for 2 hours beforehand, then rinsed and drained

½ teaspoon sweet paprika

1 tablespoon extra virgin olive oil

Preheat the oven to 220°C (425°F). Line a baking tray with baking paper.

Arrange the capsicum and tomatoes on the prepared baking tray in a single layer, drizzle with the olive oil and roast for 20 minutes until the capsicum starts to char and blacken at the edges.

Transfer to a blender or food processor, add the remaining ingredients and whiz to a pulpy consistency.

For little ones: *Try this spread on toast cut into fingers, or use as a dip for vegetable sticks or 'crudités'.*

PREPARATION TIME 10 minutes, plus 2 hours' soaking time (optional) **COOKING TIME** 20 minutes
⋙ DIETARY INFO Dairy-free ● gluten-free ● vegetarian ● vegan

Spiced Roast Carrot
and Hempseed Hummus

MAKES ABOUT 500 ML (17 FL OZ/2 CUPS)

This lightly spiced hummus is naturally sweet from the roasted carrots, and a beautiful golden yellow thanks to the soothing turmeric. It is extremely versatile, and this recipe makes a big batch that you can dip into over the week.

If you struggle to get hold of hempseeds from your local health food store, simply swap them with the same weight of an alternative seed such as sunflower.

2 large carrots, roughly chopped

2 garlic cloves, crushed

1 x 3 cm (1¼ inch) piece of fresh root ginger, peeled and crushed

1 tablespoon olive oil

250 g (9 oz/1 cup) cooked chickpeas, rinsed and drained

60 ml (2 fl oz/¼ cup) aquafaba (chickpea cooking water; see page 225)

40 g (1½ oz/¼ cup) hempseeds, plus extra, to serve

2 tablespoons extra virgin olive oil

¼ teaspoon ground turmeric

Preheat the oven to 220°C (425°F). Line a baking tray with baking paper.

Put the carrot, garlic, ginger and olive oil in a bowl, and stir to coat everything in the oil. Transfer to the prepared baking tray, making sure to scrape out any of the garlic and ginger remaining in the bowl, and roast for 15 minutes.

Tip the carrots, garlic, ginger and flavoured oil into a blender or food processor, scraping the baking paper to catch all the juices. Add the remaining ingredients, and blend until smooth. Transfer to a bowl ready to serve, and sprinkle some extra hempseeds on top.

For little ones: *Try this spread on toast cut into fingers, or use as a dip for vegetables sticks or 'crudités'.*

PREPARATION TIME 15 minutes **COOKING TIME** 15 minutes
≫ DIETARY INFO Dairy-free ● gluten-free ● nut-free ● sesame-free ● vegetarian ● vegan

Summer Berry and Coconut
Frozen Labneh Cups

MAKES ABOUT 12

In summer I like to keep a batch of these tucked away in the freezer for hungry tummies. You can use Greek-style yoghurt instead of labneh, but it is definitely worth having a go at straining yoghurt, at least overnight, for a creamier version (see page 240). Either way, straight from the freezer these can be quite crunchy. I actually like them this way, but let them sit for 15 minutes and they'll soften a bit, but still be firm enough to hold and bite into. I've added a touch of maple syrup here, to help keep the labneh soft. I also find that the berries can lose a little of their sweetness once the labneh purée is frozen. This recipe is really flexible. You can use other fruits, or prepare the base and labneh in a large, lined cake tin or baking tray. Once frozen, remove from the freezer and allow to soften for 10–15 minutes, then use a biscuit (cookie) cutter to make fun shapes, or simply cut into fingers.

50 g (1¾ oz/½ cup) rolled (porridge) oats (see note, page 104)

50 g (1¾ oz/⅓ cup) unsalted raw cashews, preferably soaked for 2 hours beforehand, then rinsed and drained

45 g (1¾ oz/⅔ cup) unsweetened shredded coconut, plus extra, to serve

10 soft medjool dates, pitted

60 ml (2 fl oz/¼ cup) coconut oil

1 tablespoon tahini

2 teaspoons carob flour

1 teaspoon chia seeds

290 g (10¼ oz/1¼ cups) labneh

125 g (4½ oz/1 cup) fresh or frozen raspberries

115 g (4 oz/¾ cup) fresh or frozen blueberries

1 tablespoon maple syrup (optional)

Line a 12-hole cupcake tin with paper cases.

Put the rolled oats, cashews, coconut, dates, coconut oil, tahini, carob flour and chia seeds in a blender or food processor, and whiz for about 30 seconds until you have a fine crumb. Divide equally between the cupcake cases, and press with your fingers to flatten. Set aside.

Using a hand-held blender, make a raspberry purée with half the labneh and a blueberry purée with the other half of the labneh. Add maple syrup to each of the purées, if you like, and stir well. Spoon the purées, one after the other, into the cupcake holes. You can swirl around the purées with a fork or layer them as you prefer. Top with a sprinkle of extra coconut.

Pop into the freezer for 3–4 hours until firm. Remove from the freezer and their cases, and allow to soften for about 15 minutes before serving.

For little ones: *These may be easier to handle if cut in half, or try my tip of making them in a baking tray and cutting into fingers for easy gripping.*

PREPARATION TIME 10 minutes, plus 2 hours' soaking (optional) **FREEZING TIME** 3–4 hours
⋙ DIETARY INFO Egg-free ● vegetarian

Blueberry and Lemon
Yoghurt Scone Fingers

MAKES 12–16 SCONES

Every day I find myself wishing I could pause the special moments that I share with my children, to completely soak them in and retain those memories for when I'm old and they're leading full lives of their own. One such example is how in the afternoons the pace of our daily rhythm slows, and I'll often retreat to the sofa with my boys. A good picture book in one hand and a little plate of warm scone fingers in the other, we make time for tea and snuggles.

200 g (7 oz/1⅓ cups) wholemeal (whole-grain) spelt flour

100 g (3½ oz/⅔ cup) unbleached white spelt flour

2 teaspoons bicarbonate of soda (baking soda)

90 g (3¼ oz) unsalted butter (preferably grass-fed), softened

60 g (2¼ oz/½ cup) oatmeal (Scottish oats/ground oats; see note on page 104)

1 ripe banana

1 egg

grated zest and juice of 2 unwaxed lemons (remove pips)

150 g (5½ oz) plain yoghurt

100 g (3½ oz/⅔ cup) fresh or frozen blueberries

Preheat the oven to 190°C (375°F). Line a baking tray with baking paper.

Sift the flours and bicarbonate of soda into a large bowl. Use your fingers to break up the butter, and rub it in until you have a texture like very fine breadcrumbs. Add the oatmeal, and mix together until it's evenly distributed. Mash the banana with a fork, and stir into the dry ingredients.

In a separate bowl, beat together the egg and lemon juice. Decant a quarter of this into a small bowl, add the lemon zest and whisk to make the glaze. Set aside.

Add the yoghurt to the remaining egg mixture, and beat well until combined. Add this to the flour–banana mixture, and bring together with a spoon or your hands until you have a soft dough. Turn out onto the prepared baking tray, and gently press until it is about 2 cm (¾ inch) thick. Spread the blueberries on top, and carefully press them in, so that just the very tops are peeping out.

Use a pastry brush to glaze the top of the scone with the egg glaze. Use all of this, even if it looks quite wet. Bake for 20 minutes until golden brown on top.

Slide the scone onto a chopping board using a palette knife, and carefully cut into 12–16 fingers while still hot. Transfer to a wire rack, and leave to cool for about 10 minutes. Serve while still warm.

For little ones: *Ensure the blueberries have cooled before serving.*

PREPARATION TIME 15 minutes **COOKING TIME** 20 minutes
≫ DIETARY INFO Nut-free ● vegetarian

Autumn

Roasting roots, picking apples, rinsing vibrant greens – the slower pace of autumn is a time to retreat under woollen blankets and enjoy Mother Nature's bounty. As the leaves fall and the days curl into themselves, pots of velvety pumpkin soup and barley stew simmer on the stove and creamy soaked oats bubble away in the oven.

Sweet Potato Hash Browns
with Baked Beans

MAKES ABOUT 16 SMALL HASH BROWNS

This makes a big pot full of beans and a plate piled high with hash browns. Both can be refrigerated or frozen for use later, so you do get a good number of helpings for your efforts. I usually fry several hash browns at once, to speed everything up.

BAKED BEANS

1 tablespoon olive oil

1 onion, finely chopped

3 garlic cloves, crushed

½ teaspoon fennel seeds

½ teaspoon cumin seeds

5 large truss tomatoes, roughly chopped

40 g (1½ oz/¼ cup) sun-dried tomatoes

4 soft medjool dates, pitted

1 teaspoon red wine vinegar (optional)

1 small handful fresh basil leaves

750 g (1 lb 10 oz/3 cups) cooked cannellini beans, rinsed and drained

HASH BROWNS

2 large sweet potatoes (about 650 g/1 lb 7 oz), peeled

10 spring onions (scallions), green part only, finely sliced

50 g (1¾ oz/⅓ cup) wholemeal (whole-grain) spelt flour

3 eggs, lightly beaten

olive oil for frying

To make the baked beans: Preheat the oven to 200°C (400°F). Heat the olive oil in a large saucepan over medium–low heat. Add the onion, garlic, fennel and cumin seeds, and sauté for about 5 minutes until softened and fragrant. Add the tomatoes, sun-dried tomatoes, dates and vinegar, if you like. Reduce the heat to medium, and cook for a further 10 minutes, stirring occasionally to prevent burning and adding the basil 5 minutes before the end of the cooking time.

Use a hand-held blender or food processor to carefully purée the sauce (it will be hot), then empty into a large ceramic ovenproof dish with the beans and give everything a good stir. Pop into the oven, and bake for 30 minutes.

To make the hash browns: Grate the sweet potato using a grater or a food processor with a grating disc. Put in a medium bowl with the spring onion, flour and eggs. Stir to combine.

Allowing 1 teaspoon olive oil per hash brown, heat the oil in a large frying pan over medium heat. Make a patty with a heaped tablespoon of the sweet potato mixture, carefully drop into the pan and flatten with a spatula into a hash brown shape. Fry for 2–4 minutes until golden brown, then flip over and repeat on the other side.

For little ones: *Mash the beans on top of the hash browns, and cut into fingers for easier gripping.*

PREPARATION TIME 20 minutes **COOKING TIME** 45 minutes

≫ DIETARY INFO Dairy-free ● gluten-free option (use gluten-free flour) ● nut-free ● vegetarian

Peachy Baked Oats
with Maple Pecan Crunch

MAKES 4 ADULT PORTIONS OR 8 BABY PORTIONS

Nourishing porridges make for cosy mornings during the cooler seasons of autumn and winter. I've kept this particular porridge simple and creamy, and ever so slightly spiced, and I adore juicy peaches baked this way. With some of the preparation happening the night before, this gives you a head start and reduces the cooking time in the morning.

190 g (6¾ oz/2 cups) rolled (porridge) oats (see note on page 104)

130 g (4½ oz/½ cup) Greek-style yoghurt

½ teaspoon ground allspice

100 g (3½ oz/1 cup) pecans

2 teaspoons maple syrup

4 ripe peaches

The night before, put 750 ml (26 fl oz/3 cups) water in a large ceramic baking dish. Add the oats, yoghurt and allspice, and stir well to combine. Cover with plastic wrap and refrigerate overnight.

On the day of cooking, preheat the oven to 200°C (400°F). Remove the oat mixture from the refrigerator and uncover.

Put the pecans and maple syrup in a blender or food processor, and pulse to obtain a crumble consistency. Sprinkle half this mixture on top of the oats, reserving the rest.

Halve your peaches by slicing around the stones, beginning at the crease on their tops. Twist and the peach should pull apart (unless you're using a clingstone variety, of course!), then remove the stone from one side by using a knife to flick it out. Try to do this over the oatmeal, to catch any juice that escapes; stir in the juice when you have finished preparing all the peaches. Nestle the peaches into the oats, cut side up. Sprinkle over the remaining pecan mixture.

Bake for 20 minutes until piping hot and the pecans are roasted. (Increase the cooking time to 30 minutes if the oats have not been soaked overnight.)

For little ones: *Try scooping out some of the peach to make a 'boat' into which you can spoon some of the oats. Otherwise, slice the peach into segments for easier gripping, and hand over a spoon pre-loaded with the porridge. Remember to pulse the pecans for a little longer, to ensure that they're finely chopped.*

PREPARATION TIME 10 minutes, plus overnight soaking **COOKING TIME** 20–30 minutes
≫ DIETARY INFO Nut-free option (omit the pecan crunch) ● vegetarian

Oat Smoothie Bowl
with Warm Spiced Chamomile

MAKES 2 ADULT PORTIONS OR 4 BABY PORTIONS

Chamomile is a gentle, calming tea traditionally used to support digestion. Here, I've infused it in a milky base, along with cinnamon, vanilla and just a pinch of nutmeg to make a light and soothing breakfast. I have topped it with almost gooey fried bananas, but stewed apples and pears could also work well – just don't go overboard. Some smoothie bowl recipes use lots of fruit in the base, then pile even more on top. While this looks pretty, it's a lot of fruit for our bodies to deal with in one go. Stick to one portion of fruit and, if you like, sprinkle over coconut, crushed nuts, or seeds such as chia or hemp, or even a drizzle of tahini.

375 ml (13 fl oz/1½ cups) milk

2 chamomile teabags or 1 tablespoon loose chamomile tea

75 g (2½ oz/¾ cup) rolled (porridge) oats (see note on page 104)

2 teaspoons maple syrup (optional)

¾ teaspoon ground cinnamon

¼ teaspoon unsweetened vanilla bean powder (ground vanilla; see page 237)

⅛ teaspoon ground nutmeg

1 tablespoon coconut oil

2 bananas

Bring the milk to the boil in a small saucepan, immediately remove from the heat, add the chamomile tea and steep for 10 minutes. Press the teabags as you remove them, and pour the infused milk into a blender or food processor. (If using loose tea, strain the hot milk through a fine-mesh sieve or strainer, pressing the leaves with the back of a spoon to catch all the chamomile flavour.)

Add the oats, maple syrup, ½ teaspoon of the ground cinnamon, vanilla bean powder and nutmeg, and blend or process until smooth. Return to the saucepan and heat gently for 5 minutes.

Heat the coconut oil in a small frying pan over medium heat. Meanwhile, peel and slice the bananas lengthways. Sprinkle the remaining cinnamon onto a plate, and rub the flat side of the banana strips in it to coat. Transfer to the frying pan, and cook for 1–2 minutes on each side.

Divide the warmed smoothie evenly between two bowls, and top with the bananas.

For little ones: *Cook the bananas only briefly, so that they're still firm enough to hold after cooling. Offer the smoothie in a small lidless cup, and support your baby as they drink it.*

PREPARATION TIME 10 minutes **COOKING TIME** 15 minutes
➸ **DIETARY INFO** Dairy-free option (use plant-based milk) ● nut-free ● vegetarian ● vegan option (use plant-based milk)

Blackberry Crumble Pots
with Almonds and Coconut

MAKES 4 ADULT PORTIONS OR 8 BABY PORTIONS

Autumn days are made for crumbles, so why not have one for breakfast? This wholesome version is full of nuts, seeds and oats, spiced with just a smidgen of ginger, sweetened with dates and a dash of maple syrup if you fancy. I remember combing the hedgerows near our home for blackberries as a child – trying ever so hard to get to the ripened ones without being scratched by any thorns. Laden with a big bag, we'd nibble on our pickings on the way home, inking our hands with the telltale purple juices. Even after our grazing, we'd usually have enough left for Mum to bake into a pie or crumble, often with any apples that came from the trees in our garden. You can prepare these the night before, and pop them in the oven in the morning once it's had a chance to wake and warm up, like you. We enjoy these with a splodge of unflavoured Greek-style yoghurt, and they also work well as a dessert. Swap in other seasonal fruit to enjoy all year round.

360 g (12¾ oz/3 cups) fresh or frozen blackberries

about 1 tablespoon maple syrup (optional)

50 g (1¾ oz/½ cup) rolled (porridge) oats (see note on page 104)

50 g (1¾ oz/⅓ cup) whole natural almonds

25 g (1 oz/¼ cup) unsweetened desiccated (finely shredded) coconut

4 soft medjool dates, pitted

2 tablespoons flaxseed meal

1 tablespoon unsalted butter (preferably grass-fed) or coconut oil, chilled

¼ teaspoon ground ginger

about 160 ml (5¼ fl oz) milk

Preheat the oven to 180°C (350°F).

Divide the blackberries equally among four ramekins, and stir about 1 teaspoon maple syrup into each one, if you like, ensuring that the berries are well coated.

Pulse the remaining ingredients except the milk in a blender or food processor for about 30 seconds until you have a crumble texture. Divide the crumble evenly among the ramekins, then spoon 2 tablespoons or so of the milk over the top of each serving, allowing it to soak through the mixture.

Sit the ramekins on a baking tray, and cover with a piece of baking paper to prevent burning. Bake for 20 minutes until slightly browned on top. Remove from the oven, and stir to mix the berries and warm milk into the crumble, turning everything a beautiful purple colour. Allow to cool a little before serving, remembering that the ramekins can be hot.

For little ones: *Empty the crumble into a fresh bowl for quicker cooling, and squash the crumble against a spoon for self-feeding.*

PREPARATION TIME 10 minutes **COOKING TIME** 20 minutes

»» **DIETARY INFO** Dairy-free option (use plant-based milk and coconut oil instead of butter) • vegetarian • vegan option (use plant-based milk and coconut oil instead of butter)

Banana and Coconut Bread
with Raspberries

MAKES 1 LOAF

Having a second baby brings back all those memories of the early days with
a newborn — when cold cups of tea and abandoned breakfasts are all too common.
It's for days like these, which are part and parcel of parenthood, that recipes such
as this one exist. Delicious hot or cold, this banana bread is a wholesome option
when you need sustenance. Unlike many banana breads, this one really does have
very little added sugar. Just a dash of maple syrup is all that's needed.

100 g (3½ oz/⅔ cup) unbleached
white spelt flour

70 g (2½ oz/½ cup) wholemeal
(whole-grain) spelt flour

90 g (3¼ oz/1 cup) unsweetened
desiccated (finely shredded) coconut

1 teaspoon unsweetened vanilla
bean powder (ground vanilla; see
page 237)

1 teaspoon aluminium-free baking
powder (see page 236)

½ teaspoon bicarbonate of soda
(baking soda)

200 g (7 oz/¾ cup) plain yoghurt

60 ml (2 fl oz/¼ cup) mild olive oil

60 ml (2 fl oz/¼ cup) milk

3 eggs

2 tablespoons maple syrup

250 g (9 oz) peeled ripe bananas
(about 2 or 3), roughly chopped

90 g (3¼ oz/¾ cup) fresh or frozen
raspberries

20 g (¾ oz/¼ cup) unsweetened
shredded coconut

Preheat the oven to 180°C (350°F). Line a deep 19 x 9 cm (7½ x
3½ inch) loaf (bar) tin with baking paper.

Put the flours, desiccated coconut, vanilla bean powder, baking
powder and bicarbonate of soda in a large bowl. Use a whisk to stir
them together well.

In a separate bowl, beat together the yoghurt, olive oil, milk, eggs
and maple syrup until smooth, then pour into the dry ingredients.
Mix until all the ingredients are incorporated and no flour is visible,
then fold in the bananas and raspberries.

Spoon the batter into the prepared baking tin, sprinkle over the
shredded coconut and gently pat this down and level the mixture
with the back of a spoon. Cover with a layer of baking paper to
prevent the coconut from burning, and bake for 50 minutes, or until
a skewer inserted into the centre comes out clean (you will need
about an hour's cooking time if using frozen raspberries).

Allow to cool in the tin for 10 minutes, then transfer to a wire rack
until cool enough to serve.

For little ones: *Cut the bread into fingers for easier gripping.*

PREPARATION TIME 15 minutes **COOKING TIME** 50–60 minutes
⫸ DIETARY INFO Nut-free ● vegetarian

Hazelnut and Rosemary Galette
with Beetroot and Caramelised Onion

MAKES 4 ADULT PORTIONS OR 8 BABY PORTIONS

An open pie is such a delightful way of serving seasonal vegetables. Here I've made the pastry autumnal with rosemary and hazelnuts, but you can easily adapt this recipe using sweet spices such as cinnamon, vanilla and a dash of maple syrup to load in stone fruits, berries or other root vegetables.

BEETROOT AND CARAMELISED ONION FILLING

1 red onion, finely sliced

1 tablespoon unsalted butter (preferably grass-fed)

2 teaspoons maple syrup

2 teaspoons wholemeal (whole-grain) spelt flour

170 ml (5½ fl oz/⅔ cup) vegetable stock

4–5 baby beetroot (beets) with their leaves, scrubbed, thick stems removed and leaves reserved

PASTRY

250 g (9 oz/1⅔ cups) wholemeal (whole-grain) spelt flour

200 g (7 oz/1¾ cups) hazelnut meal

125 ml (4 fl oz/½ cup) olive oil

2–3 tablespoons fresh rosemary leaves

1 egg, lightly beaten

Preheat the oven to 180°C (350°F). Line a large baking tray with baking paper.

To make the filling: In a small frying pan, sweat the onion with the butter and maple syrup over medium–low heat for 25 minutes, stirring occasionally to prevent burning, until very soft and caramelised. Stir in the flour and stock, and cook for a couple more minutes to thicken. Remove from the heat and set aside.

To make the pastry: Meanwhile, put the flour, hazelnut meal, olive oil and rosemary in a food processor, and whiz until fine and crumbly. Transfer to a large bowl. Add half the beaten egg and 125 ml (4 fl oz/½ cup) cold water. Using your hands, bring together into a dough. Empty onto a clean work surface, and knead for 5 minutes. Cover with plastic wrap, and refrigerate for 15 minutes.

To finish: Retrieve the pastry from the refrigerator, and roll out on the baking paper into a rough circle 5 mm–1 cm (¼–½ inch) thick. Roughly chop the beet leaves, and use to cover the centre of the pastry. Trim off both ends of the beetroot and discard. Thinly slice the flesh into rings, and arrange on top of the leaves. Fold over the sides of the pastry to make the galette, then pour over the caramelised onion. Brush the pastry with the remaining beaten egg.

Bake for 40–45 minutes until the beetroot is cooked through and soft, and the pastry golden brown.

For little ones: *The top crust can be quite firm for toothless little ones. Remove this and serve the bottom sliced into fingers.*

PREPARATION TIME 1 hour **COOKING TIME** 45 minutes
DIETARY INFO Vegetarian

Sourdough Stuffing
with Pumpkin and Sage

MAKES 4 ADULT PORTIONS OR 8 BABY PORTIONS

Serve this colourful stuffing on its own or alongside slow-cooked roasted meat.
I've kept everything really chunky here, but you can also pulse the ingredients
in a food processor and use it like a traditional stuffing in poultry or perhaps roll
it into balls or make fun shapes using a biscuit (cookie) cutter.

Wholemeal sourdough breads are our go-to choice, not just because of their
flavour. Souring (fermenting) grains is one of three traditional methods used
to make their nutrients, particularly minerals, much easier to digest and absorb
(see page 239 for more).

2 tablespoons olive oil

5 French shallots, finely chopped

800 g (1 lb 12 oz) pumpkin (winter squash), peeled, seeded and diced

4 thick slices wholemeal (whole-wheat) sourdough bread (crust left on), toasted and diced

2 eggs, lightly beaten

3 tablespoons chopped fresh sage

Preheat the oven to 200°C (400°F).

Heat the olive oil in a large frying pan over medium heat. Add
the shallot, pumpkin and bread. Cook for 10 minutes, stirring
occasionally, until the onion has softened.

Tip the stuffing into an ovenproof dish. Add the beaten egg and
sage, and season with freshly ground black pepper. Mix well and
press down with the back of the spoon to level. Bake for 30 minutes
until the pumpkin is cooked through and tender, and the bread has
slightly browned.

For little ones: *This chunky stuffing is a good option for beginners
to handle. Make sure that it has cooled down enough before
serving – it comes out of the oven piping hot.*

PREPARATION TIME 15 minutes **COOKING TIME** 40 minutes
≫ DIETARY INFO Dairy-free ● gluten-free option (use gluten-free bread) ● nut-free ● vegetarian

Orange and Tahini Baked Tofu
with Sweet Potato and Kale Chips

MAKES 4 ADULT PORTIONS AND 8 BABY PORTIONS

Although I am a strong advocate of serving one meal to the whole family, this shouldn't mean that you can't bring a little fun to small plates. Using a biscuit (cookie) cutter is a simple way of brightening up what's otherwise a rather meek-looking food – tofu, that is. Tofu is also very bland on its own and so, if I know that I'll be making baked tofu for dinner, I usually leave my tofu to press in the refrigerator overnight, then put it in the marinade in the morning.

The only fuss with this dish is shimmying around your baking trays to get all your ingredients cooked at the right time. This is fine if you have a large oven and four large baking trays, but in the real world the best way to approach this is to bake your tofu and root vegetables first, then while these are cooling (remembering that little ones will be using their hands) you can quickly do the kale chips.

---

350 g (12 oz) firm tofu

grated zest and juice of 3 unwaxed oranges (remove pips)

2 tablespoons tahini

1 x 2 cm (¾ in) piece of fresh root ginger, peeled and grated

¼ teaspoon chilli flakes

550 g (1 lb 4 oz) orange sweet potato, peeled and cut into slices 1 cm (½ inch) thick

4 radishes, halved

2 tablespoons olive oil, plus extra, to rub on the kale

400 g (14 oz) curly kale, large stems removed

seeds from 1 pomegranate

If you have a tofu press, use this; otherwise, place a couple of sheets of paper towel on a plate, rest the tofu on these, layer a couple more sheets on top, then another plate, and finish with something heavy to press out the aquafaba. I have a heavy teapot that does this job nicely, but a heavy bowl or dish also works well. Leave for at least 30 minutes (if using paper towel, it should be damp after pressing).

Meanwhile, make the marinade by whisking together the orange zest and juice, tahini, ginger and chilli flakes until combined. Note that the tahini won't mix into the orange juice as such, but you want to whisk it to a point where you have a smooth dressing. Set aside.

Slice the tofu into strips 1 cm (½ inch) thick, then again into squares, or use a biscuit (cookie) cutter to make pretty shapes. Put in a bowl with the marinade. Cover, transfer to the refrigerator and leave to rest for at least 30 minutes but several hours if possible.

Preheat the oven to 180°C (350°F).

Arrange the sweet potato and radishes on a large baking tray, keeping them spaced out slightly, and drizzle with the olive oil. Retrieve the tofu from the marinade, and spread this out on a second baking tray. Place both trays in the oven, and bake for 20–25 minutes, rotating the trays halfway through the cooking time.

Tear your kale leaves into smaller, even-sized pieces. They need to be completely dry; otherwise you'll end up steaming rather than baking them, and end up with woefully soggy chips. With about a teaspoon of olive oil in your hands, take one piece of kale at a time and gently massage the oil into the leaves until they're lightly coated. Arrange the leaves on two baking trays as you go, and apply more olive oil as needed – your hands will be wonderfully soft by the time you've finished the bunch.

Bake for 15–20 minutes until crisp. Depending on the size of your oven, you may need to swap the position of the two trays halfway through for even cooking, and do keep an eye on them, as they can go from crisp to burnt quite quickly.

Arrange the tofu, sweet potato, radish halves and kale chips on a large serving plate, sprinkle over the pomegranate seeds and drizzle over some of the marinade.

For little ones: *The pomegranate seeds will be too small for beginners to handle, so leave these out of their portion. Ensure that the radishes are very soft for beginners.*

PREPARATION TIME 1 hour 15 minutes, including pressing and marinating the tofu **COOKING TIME** 45 minutes
⟫⟫ DIETARY INFO Dairy-free ● gluten-free ● nut-free ● vegetarian ● vegan

Miso Beef, Barley and Kale Stew
with Toasted Sesame Dumplings

MAKES 4–6 ADULT PORTIONS OR 8–12 BABY PORTIONS

My mother was always able to piece together a hearty stew with very little in the way of ingredients. A good handful of barley was thrown into the stew pot, and every ladleful was brimming with flavour, making for happy, full tummies.

STEW

2 tablespoons olive oil

4 carrots, diced

2 celery stalks, finely chopped

1 onion, finely chopped

4 garlic cloves, finely chopped

500 g (1 lb 2 oz) beef (choose a lean cut such as chuck), cut into chunks

500 g (1 lb 2 oz) all-purpose potatoes, cut into chunks

70 g (2½ oz/⅓ cup) pearl barley

1 tablespoon white miso

2 tablespoons fresh rosemary leaves

1 tablespoon cornflour (cornstarch)

90 g (3¼ oz) kale

DUMPLINGS

1 teaspoon sesame oil or olive oil

2 tablespoons sesame seeds

150 g (5½ oz/1 cup) wholemeal (whole-grain) spelt or wheat flour

1 teaspoon aluminium-free baking powder (see page 236)

60 g (2¼ oz) chilled unsalted butter (preferably grass-fed)

60 ml (2 fl oz/¼ cup) milk

To make the stew: Heat the oil in a large saucepan over medium heat. Add the carrot, celery, onion and garlic, and sweat for 5 minutes to soften. Add the beef and cook for a further 5 minutes until the meat has browned. Add 2 litres (70 fl oz/8 cups) water and the potato, barley, miso and rosemary. In a small bowl, dissolve the cornflour in 1 tablespoon cold water, then add to the pan. Bring to the boil, reduce the heat to a simmer, cover and cook for 1 hour. Remove the lid and cook, uncovered, for a further 40 minutes.

Remove and discard the large stems from the kale; finely chop the leaves. Add to the stew, and arrange the prepared dumplings on top. Cover and cook for a final 20 minutes before serving.

To make the dumplings: Towards the end of the stew's cooking time, heat the oil in a small frying pan over medium–low heat. Add the sesame seeds and toast for 4–5 minutes until just starting to turn golden brown. Watch carefully, as they burn easily.

Whisk together the flour and baking powder in a large bowl until combined. Add the sesame seeds and stir through. Cut the butter into dice, and rub into the flour mixture to obtain a breadcrumb consistency. Add the milk and bring the dough together. Roll into 8–12 balls, depending on how many people you're serving and remembering that the dumplings will puff up as they steam. Cover and set aside. Add to the stew for the final 20 minutes of cooking, lid on, until they are puffed up and cooked through.

For little ones: *The meat should be soft to suck on and the vegetables chunky enough to hold. The dumplings can be cut in half for easier gripping.*

PREPARATION TIME 20 minutes **COOKING TIME** 2 hours 10 minutes
≫ DIETARY INFO Nut-free

Sweet Potato Falafel
Mini Mezze Bowl

MAKES 4 ADULT PORTIONS OR 8 BABY PORTIONS

The idea of mezze is that there is a variety of tastes and textures to pick and choose from. This is such a great idea for little ones, as it gives them more control over what and how much they want to eat.

The main part of this mini mezze is a sweet potato falafel, and to this you can add your own selection of seasonal fruit, roast vegetables, dips such as hummus (roast carrot, page 127; or beetroot, page 200) and fresh cheeses such as labneh (see page 240) or paneer. Sumac chickpeas (from the Pumpkin and Persimmon Soup with Sumac Roast Chickpeas recipe on page 161) also work well here.

---

300 g (10½ oz) orange-red sweet potato, peeled and diced

1 red onion, chopped

2 garlic cloves, peeled

500 g (1 lb 2 oz/2 cups) cooked chickpeas, rinsed and well drained

40 g (1½ oz/⅓ cup) besan (chickpea) flour

1 large handful flat-leaf (Italian) parsley leaves

1 large handful coriander (cilantro) leaves

grated zest of 1 unwaxed lemon

2 teaspoons ground cumin

1 teaspoon ground coriander

TO SERVE
a selection of dips, seasonal fruit and roast vegetables and tortillas (see page 72)

Preheat the oven to 200°C (400°F). Grease a large baking tray with olive oil.

Put the sweet potato, red onion and garlic cloves in a food processor, and pulse a few times until everything is finely chopped. Be careful not to over-process; otherwise your falafel will end up like little balls of mashed potato. Add the remaining ingredients, and pulse again until everything is well combined (you may need to scrape down the sides). Empty into a large bowl.

Use your hands to scoop the mixture, and shape into 15–20 balls or patties. As you do this, squeeze the mixture well to remove any extra liquid and ensure that the ingredients bind together as they cook. If you feel that the mix may crumble, stir in some additional besan flour at this stage. Brush or spray the falafel with extra olive oil and bake for 30 minutes.

Divide the falafel among large serving bowls, and heap in a mix of other foods to make a mini platter or bowl.

For little ones: *For beginners, I advise against serving this in an actual bowl because you'll end up with a mega mess rather than a mini mezze. Place two or three options in front of them to choose from, and go from there.*

PREPARATION TIME 20 minutes **COOKING TIME** 30 minutes
➤➤➤ **DIETARY INFO** Dairy-free (omit fresh cheeses) ● gluten-free ● nut-free ● vegetarian ● vegan (omit fresh cheeses)

Lemony Paprika Poached Chicken
with Broccoli and Pasta

MAKES 4 ADULT PORTIONS OR 8 BABY PORTIONS

This creamy pasta is a gem for weeknights. It takes no time at all to bring together, and I can leave it bubbling away on the stove as I recover from a busy day. This is also a good recipe to double up on the ingredients and make a large batch, so that you can freeze some for later.

1 tablespoon olive oil

1 red onion, quartered

1 garlic clove, crushed

2 tablespoons tomato paste (concentrated purée)

2 teaspoons sweet paprika

¼ teaspoon ground turmeric

grated zest of 2 unwaxed lemons (remove pips)

2 organic free-range skinless chicken breast fillets (about 500 g/1 lb 2 oz), sliced

400 ml (14 fl oz) coconut milk

300 g (10½ oz/5 cups) broccoli florets

200 g (7 oz/2¼ cups) wholemeal (whole-wheat) pasta

Heat the olive oil in a medium saucepan over medium heat, and gently fry the onion and garlic for 5 minutes until softened. Add the tomato paste, spices, lemon zest and chicken, and stir so the meat is completely coated. Pour in the coconut milk, and bring to the boil. Reduce the heat to low, and simmer, uncovered, for 30 minutes.

Meanwhile, steam or boil the broccoli until tender, and prepare the pasta according to the packet instructions. Empty into a serving dish, and combine with the poached chicken and sauce when cooked. Serve warm.

For little ones: *This is a really good first finger food to try when your baby is around 6 months old. The chicken is poached and so very soft, and the broccoli and pasta are easy to handle.*

PREPARATION TIME 10 minutes **COOKING TIME** 35 minutes
»» DIETARY INFO Dairy-free ● gluten-free option (use gluten-free pasta) ● nut-free

Golden Fish Fingers
with Buttery Potatoes and Carrots

MAKES 4–6 ADULT PORTIONS OR 8–12 BABY PORTIONS

Fish fingers (fish sticks) are easy enough to make at home once you have a production line going, and it's really easy to involve children by putting them in charge of the flour, egg or crumb stations. This recipe will make a big stack of fish fingers and so, if you've used fresh fish, you can always freeze the fingers after they have been crumbed and save them for cooking at a later date. It's worth noting that any flour will work to coat the fish; it's just there to help the egg and crumb stick.

180 g (6 oz/1½ cups) oatmeal (Scottish oats/ground oats; see note on page 104)

50 g (1¾ oz/½ cup) finely grated parmesan cheese

40 g (1½ oz/¼ cup) pine nuts, crushed

4 garlic cloves, crushed

grated zest and juice of 1 unwaxed lemon (remove pips)

4 sustainably caught skinless and boneless firm fish fillets (500 g/ 1 lb 2 oz), sliced into 3 x 8 cm (1¼ x 3¼ inch) fingers

150 g (5½ oz/1 cup) unbleached plain (all-purpose) flour

2 eggs, lightly beaten

300 g (10½ oz) kipfler or other small new potatoes, halved

6 multicoloured carrots, cut into thin matchsticks

30 g (1 oz) unsalted butter (preferably grass-fed), melted

1 large handful mixed herbs such as flat-leaf (Italian) parsley and coriander (cilantro) leaves

Preheat the oven to 200°C (400°F). Line a baking tray with baking paper.

Combine the oatmeal, parmesan cheese, pine nuts, garlic and lemon zest in a large bowl, and toss well to mix. Set aside.

Put the flour and egg in two separate bowls. Season the flour with a little freshly ground black pepper. Set up your production line – from the left to the right you have your fish, the bowl of flour, the bowl of beaten egg, the bowl of crumb mixture and then the prepared baking tray. Dip each piece of fish into the flour, then the egg and then the crumb. Pat down to coat the fish fingers well on all sides. Space out evenly on the baking tray. Bake for 15–20 minutes, flipping halfway through the cooking time. The fish should be cooked through, opaque and flaky.

Meanwhile, boil or steam the potatoes and carrots for 15–20 minutes until softened (you can steam the carrots over the boiling potatoes).

Blend the butter, herbs and lemon juice using a hand-held blender or food processor, then mix into the cooked vegetables. Serve warm with the fish fingers.

For little ones: *This is a great dish to try for beginners, as everything is a really good shape to grip. Break the fish fingers into large pieces, and carefully check for stray little bones in the fish before serving.*

PREPARATION TIME 25 minutes **COOKING TIME** 20 minutes
⋙ DIETARY INFO Dairy-free option (use olive oil instead of butter) ● nut-free

Sweet Potato Skins Stuffed
with Creamy Salmon and Sprouts

MAKES 4 ADULT PORTIONS OR 8 BABY PORTIONS

Don't let the cooking time for this recipe fool you into thinking that making this is a chore. Baked sweet potatoes really do look after themselves, and need little more than the timer to be set so that they don't get cremated while you're distracted tending to other things.

Salmon is a quick and wholesome option that you can rustle up when the potatoes are nearly ready, and I've shredded the brussels sprouts to provide an alternative to the soggy overcooked versions you may have been unlucky enough to sample as a child (I'm looking at you, Mum.).

4 orange–red sweet potatoes (about 500 g/1 lb 2 oz)

1 tablespoon coconut oil, melted

1 tablespoon sesame oil

juice of 1 lemon (remove pips)

2 sustainably caught skinless, boneless salmon fillets (about 250 g/9 oz)

200 g (7 oz) brussels sprouts

160 ml (5¼ fl oz) coconut cream

2 tablespoons roughly chopped coriander (cilantro) leaves

1 teaspoon sesame seeds (optional)

Preheat the oven to 200°C (400°F). Line a baking tray with baking paper.

Scrub and prick the sweet potatoes, and brush with the coconut oil. Roast for about 1 hour until cooked through but not overcooked – if they're too soft, they will not hold their shape.

When the sweet potatoes are nearly finished, heat the sesame oil in a large frying pan over medium heat. Add the lemon juice and salmon, and fry for about 8 minutes until the salmon is cooked through and can be flaked.

Meanwhile, prepare the brussels sprouts by slicing off the stalk ends, then chop the sprouts in half. Finely slice each half, then add to the salmon and cook for a further 4 minutes until softened.

Remove the sweet potatoes from the oven, and carefully scoop out their soft centres. Add this soft mash along with the coconut cream and coriander to the pan with the salmon and sprouts, and stir through. Load the filling into the sweet potato skins, sprinkle over the sesame seeds, if you like, and serve.

For little ones: *Keep some of the salmon in larger chunks for easier handling and check them for any little bones. Slice the potato into fingers for easier gripping.*

PREPARATION TIME 15 minutes **COOKING TIME** 1 hour
DIETARY INFO Dairy-free ● gluten-free ● nut-free

Cauliflower Kitchari
with Mung Beans and Quinoa

MAKES 4–6 ADULT PORTIONS OR 8–12 BABY PORTIONS

Kitchari, meaning 'mixture' or 'mess', is a porridge-like stew that is a traditional first food of babies in India. It stems from Ayurvedic medicine, where it has been revered since ancient times for being nutritious and easily digested. Usually, water, rice and dried mung beans are added to a base of spices. I've swapped the rice with quinoa in my version, and made it sweeter and creamier using some coconut milk, but you can use all stock or all water, as is customary. You can also use any seasonal vegetables of your choice in place of the cauliflower, and make this a simple one-pot meal for any time of the year.

2 tablespoons ghee or coconut oil

1 red onion, finely chopped

2 garlic cloves, finely chopped

2 teaspoons cumin seeds

1 teaspoon fennel seeds

1 teaspoon black mustard seeds

2 teaspoons ground turmeric

2 teaspoons ground coriander

2 litres (70 fl oz/8 cups) vegetable stock

400 ml (14 fl oz) coconut milk

150 g (5½ oz/¾ cup) quinoa, well rinsed and drained

150 g (5½ oz/⅔ cup) whole dried mung beans, well rinsed, drained and picked over

350 g (12 oz/about 3 cups) cauliflower florets

1 bay leaf

roughly chopped fresh coriander (cilantro) leaves, to serve

Melt the ghee in a large saucepan over medium heat. Add the onion, garlic and cumin, fennel and mustard seeds, and gently fry for 5 minutes, stirring regularly. Add the ground turmeric and ground coriander. Stir to coat the onion thoroughly in the spices. Cook for a further 2 minutes until aromatic.

Pour in the stock and coconut milk, and add the quinoa, mung beans, cauliflower and bay leaf. Bring to the boil, then reduce the heat to low and simmer, covered, for 45 minutes. Retrieve the bay leaf before serving, and finish with fresh coriander scattered over the top. Serve warm.

For little ones: *Keep some of the cauliflower florets quite large, with long stems for easier gripping – there should be no issue with them cooking, as the mung beans need time to soften and split. For beginners, serve this with chapattis (see page 188) or naan bread (see page 118) for easier dipping, and finely chop and stir through the coriander.*

PREPARATION TIME 10 minutes **COOKING TIME** 65 minutes

≫ DIETARY INFO Dairy-free ● gluten-free ● nut-free ● vegetarian ● vegan option (use coconut oil not ghee)

Pumpkin and Persimmon Soup
with Sumac Roast Chickpeas

MAKES 4 ADULT PORTIONS OR 8 BABY PORTIONS

This wholly plant-powered soup is incredibly warming and perfect for autumn days. The soup gains sweetness from the persimmon and paprika, and it is topped with crispy toasted goodness from the chickpeas.

---

250 g (9 oz/1 cup) cooked chickpeas

80 ml (2½ fl oz/⅓ cup) olive oil

2 teaspoons sumac (see note)

1 red onion, roughly chopped

2 garlic cloves, roughly chopped

1 x 2 cm (¾ inch) piece of fresh root ginger, peeled and roughly chopped

1 teaspoon sweet paprika

500 g (1 lb 2 oz) peeled and seeded pumpkin (winter squash), cut into chunks

400 g (14 oz) persimmons (about 2), trimmed and cut into 2 cm (¾ inch) dice

1 litre (35 fl oz/4 cups) vegetable stock

Preheat the oven to 220°C (425°C).

Rinse and drain the chickpeas. Pat dry as much as possible with two clean tea towels (dish towels), or use a salad spinner. Empty into a large bowl with half the olive oil and the sumac, and stir to coat. Spread out over a large baking tray, drizzling over any oil remaining in the bowl, and roast for 20–25 minutes until crispy. Remove from the oven and set aside.

Meanwhile, heat the remaining olive oil in a large saucepan over medium heat. Add the onion, garlic and ginger, and sauté for 5 minutes to soften. Next, add the sweet paprika and stir to coat the onion. Cook for a further 5 minutes until aromatic. Lastly, add the pumpkin and persimmon, and pour over the stock. Bring to the boil, then reduce the heat to low and simmer, uncovered, for 15–20 minutes until the pumpkin has softened.

Remove from the heat and carefully purée with a hand-held blender. Alternatively, when the soup has cooled down sufficiently, transfer to a blender or food processor, and pulse a few times until smooth, letting any steam escape; reheat gently if needed.

Ladle into bowls, and top with the roasted chickpeas.

For little ones: *Crunchy chickpeas are a choking hazard for beginners, so blend their chickpeas into the soup before serving. Roasted chickpeas can be kept in the refrigerator for children to snack on during the day; toss them through a salad or use them in a wrap.*

Note: *Sumac, made from the crushed dried berries of a small shrub, is used as a seasoning. It brings a tart, lemony flavour to dishes.*

PREPARATION TIME 10 minutes **COOKING TIME** 30 minutes
≫ DIETARY INFO Dairy-free ● gluten-free ● nut-free ● vegetarian ● vegan

Mulled Apple Chutney
with Figs and Blackberries

MAKES ABOUT 500 ML (17 FL OZ/2 CUPS)

I love making this simple chutney when it's cold and damp outside because it fills my home with the botanical smells of sweet mulling spices. This will need refrigerating, as there is no added sugar or vinegar to preserve the fruit – but that's no matter because a jar does not last long at all. This chutney is very versatile and can be served with both sweet and savoury dishes – we like to heap it on porridge or pancakes.

500 g (1 lb 2 oz) eating apples (about 3), cored and diced

175 g (6 oz/1 cup) diced figs (from about 3 figs)

130 g (4½ oz/1 cup) fresh or frozen blackberries

grated zest and juice of 1 unwaxed orange (remove pips)

1 x 2 cm (¾ inch) piece of fresh root ginger, crushed

1 Chinese star anise (see note)

3 allspice berries

Put all the ingredients in a medium saucepan over medium heat. Bring to a gentle simmer, cover and cook for 1 hour. Transfer to a clean jar with a tight-fitting lid, and allow to cool with the lid off.

Once the chutney is cool, screw on the lid tightly, keep refrigerated and use within 3 days.

For little ones: *Spread the chutney on toast, then cut the toast into fingers, or mix into yoghurt or porridge.*

Note: *Make sure that the star anise you use is culinary Chinese star anise, rather than the closely related Japanese star anise. Although it looks very similar when dried (almost the same, in fact), Japanese star anise is toxic when consumed, particularly to babies and children, and should not be eaten.*

PREPARATION TIME 15 minutes **COOKING TIME** 1 hour
≫ **DIETARY INFO** Dairy-free ● gluten-free ● nut-free ● vegetarian ● vegan

Garlicky Roast Parsnip, Pepita and Kale Dip

MAKES ABOUT 250 ML (9 FL OZ/1 CUP)

This spread is well suited to warding off vampires, so do go easy on the garlic if you're not a true fan! We use this as a base for sandwiches and wraps, or add a dollop to our soup bowls. It's also really nice on the side of savoury dishes as a flavoursome mash.

---

400 g (14 oz) parsnips (about 3), chopped

olive oil for roasting

½ whole garlic bulb

40 g (1½ oz/¼ cup) pepitas (pumpkin seeds), preferably soaked for 8 hours beforehand, then rinsed and drained

90 g (3¼ oz) curly kale, large stems removed and roughly chopped

60 ml (2 fl oz/¼ cup) extra virgin olive oil

juice of ½ lemon (remove pips)

1 tablespoon tahini

Preheat the oven to 220°C (425°F).

Spread out the parsnips on a baking tray, and drizzle with olive oil. Slice the top off the garlic, and rub the bulb with some olive oil. Place on the baking tray with the parsnips. Roast for 20–25 minutes until softened and the parsnips have started to turn a golden brown at the edges. Sprinkle the pepitas in a single layer on the tray 5 minutes before the end of the cooking time.

Meanwhile, bring a large saucepan of water to the boil. Place a colander in the sink ready for the kale. Blanch the kale for a minute in the boiling water, then immediately rinse under cold water to stop any further cooking.

Put the kale in a blender or food processor. Add the roasted ingredients, including the garlic cloves slipped from its skins. Next, add the extra virgin olive oil, lemon juice and tahini, and pulse until you have a thick pulpy texture. You may need to scrape down the sides once or twice. If not being used at once, this can be stored in an airtight container in the refrigerator for up to 3 days.

For little ones: *A good way to try some leafy power greens. Try this spread on toast or as a dip for some lightly cooked carrot or apple.*

PREPARATION TIME 10 minutes, plus 8 hours' soaking time (optional) **COOKING TIME** 25 minutes
⫸ DIETARY INFO Dairy-free ● gluten-free ● nut-free ● vegetarian ● vegan

Apple and Date Cake
with Coconut and Cardamom

MAKES 8 ADULT PORTIONS OR 16 BABY PORTIONS

Just the sight of this simple cake emerging from the oven will be enough to warm you through on a cold autumn day. I haven't added any extra sugar to this recipe, as I find there's plenty enough natural sweetness coming from the cardamom, coconut and dates, as well as the apple slices burrowed in just so. Serve the cake still warm from the oven with some plain yoghurt and the last of the seasonal berries.

330 ml (11¼ fl oz/1⅓ cups) milk

8 soft medjool dates, pitted

10 green cardamom pods

150 g (5½ oz/1 cup) wholemeal (whole-grain) spelt flour

90 g (3¼ oz/1 cup) unsweetened desiccated (finely shredded) coconut

1½ teaspoons aluminium-free baking powder (see page 236)

2 eggs

80 ml (2½ fl oz/⅓ cup) coconut oil, melted and cooled

2 unwaxed eating apples

coconut milk powder or icing (confectioners') sugar, to dust (optional)

Preheat the oven to 180°C (350°F). Line a 19 cm (7½ inch) round cake tin or pie dish with baking paper.

Make a fragrant milk base by simmering the milk, dates and cardamom in a small saucepan over medium–low heat for 10 minutes to soften and infuse. Remove from the heat and transfer to a blender or food processor, or a jug, to cool a little while you prepare the other ingredients.

Whisk together the flour, coconut and baking powder in a large bowl until well combined.

Whiz the milk base ingredients in the blender or food processor for about 1 minute until smooth. Pour into the dry ingredients. In a separate, medium bowl, beat together the eggs and coconut oil until smooth, and add to the dry ingredients and milk base. Use a spoon to gently combine the ingredients until no flour is visible. Set aside to thicken while you prepare the apples.

Core, halve and finely slice the apples. Pour the batter into the prepared cake tin or pie dish, and evenly arrange the apple slices, peel side up, gently pushing them into the mixture.

Bake for 40 minutes. Leave to cool in the tin or dish, and dust with coconut milk powder or icing sugar, if you like, when ready to serve. This cake is best served still warm from the oven.

For little ones: *The apple slices should be soft enough for babies to suck on – you can slice them a little thicker for beginners, to allow for easier gripping.*

PREPARATION TIME 15 minutes **COOKING TIME** 50 minutes
⋙ DIETARY INFO Dairy-free option (use plant-based milk) ● nut-free ● vegetarian

Baked Vanilla Bean Labneh
with Thyme and Figs

MAKES 4 ADULT PORTIONS OR 8 BABY PORTIONS

I remember how as children we would always joke about having a special tummy just for 'afters'. We'd insist that our bellies were completely stuffed with the stew and squashed sandwiches that our mother would heap in the middle of the table, but there was always room for dessert. After all, we were anatomically designed that way.

I joke, but nutritious desserts and snacks are so important to supply little tummies with the nutrients they need for optimal growth and development. They need not be referred as treats, rewards or 'sometimes foods', and actually, if they're wholesome, who's to say they need to come second, anyway?

Potted baked labneh is very simple to prepare and is a bit of a cross between firm custard and a cheesecake. It will rise in the oven, then deflate and soften as it cools. You could use any other seasonal fruits for this – apples, blackberries, pears, persimmons and poached quince work really well. Simply leave out the thyme, as I think this is a special twist just for the juicy, fragrant figs.

410 g (14½ oz) labneh
(see page 240)

4 eggs

1 tablespoon maple syrup

½ teaspoon unsweetened vanilla bean powder (ground vanilla; see page 237)

1 tablespoon fresh thyme leaves

2 figs, halved lengthways

Preheat the oven to 180°C (350°F).

Put the labneh, eggs, maple syrup, vanilla and thyme leaves in a medium bowl, and beat together until the mixture has a smooth consistency like mayonnaise. Divide evenly among four ramekins.

Gently press a fig half, cut side up, into the labneh mixture in each ramekin. Bake for 25 minutes until cooked through and risen. Adults can enjoy this straight from the ramekin, but as these are hot you may prefer to scoop it out and transfer to a cold dish for babies and children.

For little ones: *Remove from the ramekin to cool, then slice into fingers for easy gripping. You may also want to cut the fig in half once again – it will be soft and juicy once baked, making it easy for your little one to suck out the soft flesh.*

PREPARATION TIME 10 minutes **COOKING TIME** 25 minutes
DIETARY INFO Gluten-free ● nut-free ● vegetarian

Winter

Poaching pears, roasting potatoes, popping cranberries, juicing mandarins ... Winter means paring things down and nestling in for the short days and long nights. A time to draw comfort from quinoa bakes and nourishing dals, and a ball of fudgy ice cream resting on the tippy-top of a stack of gingerbread pancakes.

Kale Shakshuka
with Sun-dried Tomatoes

MAKES 4 ADULT PORTIONS OR 8 BABY PORTIONS

Shakshuka originates from North Africa and the Middle East, where it's enjoyed particularly during the winter months. Eggs are traditionally poached in a spicy tomato sauce, but there's nothing better than a hearty bowl full of greens in the morning to revive a tired soul, and so I have really ramped up the leaves here.

This recipe calls for four eggs, but do add more if you have some hungry tummies to fill. Tear off a chunk of wholesome sourdough bread, and use this to mop up the sauce and runny egg.

150 g (5½ oz) curly kale, with large stems removed

2 garlic cloves

½ green chilli, seeded

½ teaspoon ground cumin

½ teaspoon sweet paprika

2 tablespoons almond meal

4 large tomatoes, quartered

3–4 sun-dried tomatoes

4 eggs

1 small handful coriander (cilantro) leaves, roughly chopped

wholemeal (whole-grain) sourdough bread, to serve

Preheat the oven to 200°C (400°F).

Pulse all ingredients except the eggs, coriander and bread in a food processor for about 30 seconds until the kale is finely chopped. Transfer to a large ovenproof frying pan or ceramic baking dish.

Use a spoon to part the thick sauce and make little hollows into which the eggs can nestle as you carefully break in the eggs, keeping them separate and the yolks unbroken. Bake for 25 minutes, or until cooked through.

Scatter over the coriander, and serve with the chunky bread.

For little ones: Ensure that your baby's egg is cooked through rather than runny, and finely chop the coriander or blend this into the sauce along with the other ingredients.

PREPARATION TIME 10 minutes **COOKING TIME** 25 minutes
≫ DIETARY INFO Dairy-free ● gluten-free option (use gluten-free bread) ● vegetarian

Gingerbread Pancakes
with Fudgy Tahini Ice Cream

MAKES 10–12 PANCAKES

This recipe is handy because it really can work all year round. I've filed it under winter just because that's where gingerbread, in my English heart, lives – along with nutcrackers and big knitted stockings hung on the mantelpiece. And so, for me, making gingerbread pancakes is a ritual saved especially for the festive holidays and belongs with all the other little things we do for our children that make that time as a family so magical and memorable.

Making instant ice cream is an especially useful way to use up bananas that are just on the turn; simply peel them, slice into coins or chunks, and pop into a container in the freezer. Dip into your banana stash as and when you need them, and use other ingredients to add extra flavour.

GINGERBREAD PANCAKES

310 ml (10¾ fl oz/1¼ cups) milk

4 soft medjool dates, pitted

150 g (5½ oz/1 cup) wholemeal (whole-grain) spelt flour

50 g (1¾ oz/½ cup) nut meal, such as almond or hazelnut

3 teaspoons ground ginger

1 teaspoon ground cinnamon

pinch of ground cloves

1 teaspoon aluminium-free baking powder

2 eggs

coconut oil for frying

To make the pancakes: Put the milk and dates in a small saucepan over low heat. Gently bring to a simmer, and keep simmering for a further 5 minutes to soften. Using a hand-held blender, purée the dates into the milk until smooth. Empty into a jug and set aside to cool a little.

Put all the dry ingredients in a large bowl, and whisk until evenly mixed. Beat the eggs into the date milk, then pour into the dry ingredients. Whisk to combine.

Heat 1 tablespoon coconut oil in a large frying pan over medium heat for 2–3 minutes. (It's important to get your oil hot but not smoking; otherwise the pancakes can stick to the pan.) Allow 2–3 tablespoons of the batter per pancake. Gently fry for about 3 minutes on each side until cooked through.

TAHINI ICE CREAM

80 ml (2½ fl oz/⅓ cup) milk

5 soft medjool dates, pitted

65 g (2¼ oz/¼ cup) tahini

2 tablespoons cashew butter

2 large ripe bananas, peeled and sliced into coins, frozen overnight in an airtight container

½ teaspoon unsweetened vanilla bean powder (ground vanilla)

To make the ice cream: Make the tahini fudge first by using a hand-held blender or food processor to purée the milk and dates together until smooth. Stir in the tahini and cashew butter, and set aside.

Whiz the frozen bananas and vanilla bean powder in a food processor for 2–3 minutes until you have a smooth ice-cream consistency. You'll need to stop every so often to scrape down the sides and make sure that the banana is whizzing round properly.

Combine the ice cream and fudge in a separate bowl or the container the banana was stored in overnight (as it will still be cold). Stir gently to swirl the ingredients together. The ice cream will be soft for serving straight away, or you can pop it back in the freezer to firm up a little if you prefer.

For little ones: *Cut the pancakes into fingers for easier gripping, and dip into soft ice cream. Or try using a biscuit (cookie) cutter to make fun gingerbread people.*

PREPARATION TIME 20 minutes, plus overnight freezing **COOKING TIME** 20 minutes

≫ DIETARY INFO Dairy-free option (use plant-based milk) • vegetarian

Blood Orange Skillet Cake
with Oats and Almonds

MAKES 4–6 ADULT PORTIONS OR 8–12 BABY PORTIONS

Cake for breakfast may sound the opposite of nourishing, but when you look at what I've used here – wholesome oats, almond, spelt, olive oil, milk and yoghurt, and just a splash of maple syrup for sweetness – you can see that it's entirely possible to make one that's honestly nutritious. Prepare the dry ingredients the night before, leaving just the wet ingredients to ready in the morning. Serve warm from the oven, with some plain yoghurt and perhaps some frozen berries, which we consume in plentiful amounts out of season.

70 g (2½ oz/½ cup) wholemeal (whole-grain) spelt flour

70 g (2½ oz/⅔ cup) rolled (porridge) oats (see note on page 104)

50 g (1¾ oz/½ cup) almond meal

1½ teaspoons aluminium-free baking powder (see page 236)

½ teaspoon ground cinnamon

¼ teaspoon ground ginger

¼ teaspoon unsweetened vanilla bean powder (ground vanilla; see page 237)

2 unwaxed blood oranges

2 eggs

130 g (4½ oz/½ cup) plain or Greek-style yoghurt

60 ml (2 fl oz/¼ cup) milk

60 ml (2 fl oz/¼ cup) mild olive oil, plus extra for greasing

2 tablespoons maple syrup

2 tablespoons almond flakes

Preheat the oven to 200°C (400°C). Grease a 23 cm (9 in) ovenproof frying pan with olive oil, and set aside.

In a large bowl, whisk the flour, oats, almond meal, baking powder, spices and the grated zest of both oranges until thoroughly mixed.

In a second bowl or jug, beat the wet ingredients including the juice of one of the oranges (remove any pips first), and pour this into the dry ingredients. Use a spatula or metal spoon to gently stir until the flour is no longer visible. Pour into the prepared pan.

Segment the remaining orange by slicing off the top and bottom. Using a paring knife, remove the peel in strips from top to bottom. Carefully insert the knife into one side of a segment towards the centre of the orange; repeat on the other side. Remove the segment, leaving just the bitter pith, and repeat for the other segments. Remove any pips. Arrange in the centre of the cake mixture, slightly overlapping in the middle to create a flower. Sprinkle the flaked almonds around the edge of the cake. Bake for 20–25 minutes until the top is golden brown and the almonds soft and lightly toasted.

Carefully remove the pan from the oven, as it will be very hot. Allow the cake to cool a little in the pan before serving.

For little ones: *Leave a section of the cake free of the flaked almonds for toothless little ones.*

PREPARATION TIME 15 minutes **COOKING TIME** 25 minutes
»» DIETARY INFO Vegetarian

Figgy Bircher Muesli
with Hasselback-style Apples

MAKES 8–10 ADULT PORTIONS OR 16–20 BABY PORTIONS

Sometimes I wonder what I did with all that carefree spare time in my life before children. Life with two little ones is wonderful, of course, but also tiring and hectic, and mornings can be especially so. Anything that can induce calmness and revive my soul after a broken night's sleep is welcome. Bircher muesli is perfect for weary parents – entirely nourishing, delicious and fuss-free. Your future self will thank you for taking a few minutes to prep it before bed. This makes a big batch that will do for more than one breakfast. You can skip the overnight soaking if you forget or are simply too desperate to rest. Soaking grains, nuts, seeds and legumes does make some of their nutrients more accessible to our bodies, so I try to do this as much as possible. Otherwise, enjoy this muesli as is, with warm or cold milk, or plain yoghurt. The apples take no time to prepare – as long as it takes to brew a decent cup of tea – and are deliciously warm, soft and naturally sweet.

BIRCHER MUESLI

160 g (5¾ oz/1 cup) whole natural almonds or skinless hazelnuts

400 g (14 oz/4 cups) rolled (porridge) oats (see note on page 104)

185 g (6½ oz/1 cup) preservative-free dried figs

90 g (3¼ oz/1 cup) unsweetened desiccated (finely shredded) coconut

1 teaspoon ground cinnamon

peeled and grated eating apple (allow ½ apple per adult portion)

milk (allow 125 ml/4 fl oz/ ½ cup milk per adult portion)

HASSELBACK-STYLE APPLES

1 eating apple per adult portion

coconut oil, melted, for baking

To make the muesli: Pulse the nuts, oats, figs, coconut and cinnamon in a food processor to your desired consistency. If making for little ones, pulse the nuts on their own to ensure that they're well chopped, before adding the other muesli ingredients.

Allow 1–2 large handfuls muesli per adult portion, and place this in a large bowl with the appropriate amount of grated apple and milk. Stir, cover and refrigerate overnight.

To make the Hasselback-style apples: Preheat the oven to 200°C (400°F). Line a baking tray with baking paper.

Core the apples, then halve to make two 'bridges'. Use a paring knife to make slits in the top of the apple, scoring through the peel and into the flesh, leaving a small join at the bottom so that the apple does not fall apart. Place on the baking tray, brush with coconut oil and bake for 15–20 minutes until soft. Sit on top of the muesli to serve.

For little ones: *Bircher muesli should stick to a spoon or clump together well enough for a baby to try hand-feeding.*

PREPARATION TIME 10 minutes, plus overnight soaking **COOKING TIME** 20 minutes
⋙ DIETARY INFO Dairy-free option (use plant-based milk) ● vegetarian ● vegan option (use plant-based milk)

Quinoa and Coconut Porridge
with Hibiscus-poached Orchard Fruits

MAKES 4 ADULT PORTIONS OR 8 BABY PORTIONS

If you're looking for a wholesome alternative to the popular infant rice cereals that are often chosen as a first food, then this is worth a go. This creamy, light and nourishing porridge uses a simple base of soaked quinoa flakes, with coconut and vanilla added for natural sweetness. The poached fruits are deliciously soft, and the hibiscus gives them a radiant pink hue. If you have reusable cloth teabags, these would come in handy to contain the tea leaves in the saucepan, but you can manage easily enough without them.

PORRIDGE

200 g (7 oz) quinoa flakes

750 ml (26 fl oz/3 cups) milk

45 g (1½ oz/½ cup) unsweetened desiccated (finely shredded) coconut

¼ teaspoon unsweetened vanilla bean powder (ground vanilla; see page 237)

HIBISCUS-POACHED FRUIT

2 eating apples, peeled, cored and quartered

2 pears, peeled, cored and quartered

2 tablespoons loose hibiscus tea

To make the porridge: Put the quinoa flakes and 500 ml (17 fl oz/2 cups) of the milk in a medium saucepan, and stir well. Cover and leave in the refrigerator overnight to soak.

When ready to cook, mix in the coconut, vanilla bean powder and the remaining milk. Heat for 10 minutes, uncovered, over low heat, stirring occasionally to prevent burning. Divide among four bowls, and top with the poached fruit.

To make the hibiscus-poached fruit: Put the fruit and hibiscus tea leaves in a small saucepan, and add just enough cold water to cover. Bring to the boil, then reduce the heat to low and simmer for 15 minutes. Drain, then rinse off any hibiscus leaves with warm water.

For little ones: This porridge is really sticky and so is a great option for self-feeding from a spoon or straight off the high chair.

Note: Hibiscus tea is a herbal tea made from the dried calyces (sepals) of roselle flowers. It is available from good supermarkets, specialty grocers and wholefood outlets. Try to look for organic hibiscus tea if you can.

PREPARATION TIME 10 minutes, plus overnight soaking **COOKING TIME** 15 minutes

⇛ DIETARY INFO Dairy-free option (use plant-based milk) ● gluten-free ● nut-free ● vegetarian ● vegan option (use plant-based milk)

Mandarin Panzanella
with Root Veg and Butterbeans

MAKES 4–6 ADULT PORTIONS OR 8–12 BABY PORTIONS

This beautiful winter bread salad is abundant with colour and sweet flavours, and is so easy to pull together with just a few bunches of root vegetables and a hunk of stale bread. Serve it still warm from the oven, and don't worry about cutlery – this is finger food at its best!

125 ml (4 fl oz/½ cup) extra virgin olive oil, plus extra for roasting

juice of 2 oranges (remove pips)

5 tablespoons lemon thyme leaves

300 g (10½ oz) stale wholemeal (whole-wheat) sourdough bread, diced

200 g (7 oz/1 cup) cooked butterbeans, rinsed and drained

300 g (10½ oz) mandarins (about 3), peeled and segmented

150 g (5½ oz) baby (Dutch) carrots, scrubbed and tops removed

300 g (10½ oz) baby beetroot, scrubbed and tops removed (halve any of the larger ones)

4 radishes, scrubbed and tops removed (halve any larger ones)

olive oil for roasting

2 large handfuls seasonal leafy greens such as buttered beetroot (beet) or kale leaves or baby English spinach

Preheat the oven to 200°C (400°F).

Use a blender to process the olive oil, orange juice and lemon thyme into a smooth dressing. Reserve half and set aside, and pour the remainder into a large bowl. Add the bread and butterbeans, and stir with a spoon to coat. Set aside.

Spread out the mandarins, carrots, beetroot and radishes on a large baking tray and drizzle with olive oil. On a second large baking tray, spread out the bread and butterbeans, including any dressing from the bowl. Place both trays in the oven, with the vegetables on the higher shelf, and roast for 15–20 minutes until the vegetables are soft.

Transfer the vegetables, bread and butterbeans to a large serving dish or tray, add the leafy greens and toss through the remaining dressing.

For little ones: *Although the leafy greens will be a challenge for any toothless little ones, the remaining vegetables, fruit and bread should be easy enough for beginners to have a go. Try mashing some of the soft butterbeans onto the bread or slice in half lengthways to make them easier to handle, and ensure that the root vegetables are soft.*

PREPARATION TIME 20 minutes **COOKING TIME** 20 minutes
⟫ DIETARY INFO Dairy-free ● gluten-free option (use gluten-free bread) ● nut-free ● vegetarian ● vegan

Snail Bread with Spinach
and Almond Pesto

MAKES 12 ROLLS

My mother once told me that, when she was at home with the four of us, she felt it a triumph if she was dressed by 10 a.m. I often smile when I think of that. Especially on those mornings when I marvel upon the bird's nest that my hair has become overnight and my attractive breakfast-encrusted pyjamas. There's nothing like motherhood to keep you humble, after all.

As part of our daily rhythm, I do always try to make myself reasonably presentable to the big wide world and get outside, though, and I believe this to be especially important in winter. These snail bread rolls are so perfect for packing up and taking out on an adventure. For all intents and purposes, they can be a meal on their own, but we also enjoy them dipped in soup.

The pesto recipe will yield about twice as much is needed, and that's intentional, to give you an extra batch that you can store for later. Simply cover the pesto with a thin layer of olive oil in an airtight container; keep refrigerated for up to 5 days.

SNAIL BREAD DOUGH

150 g (5½ oz/1 cup) white spelt flour

150 g (5½ oz/1 cup) wholemeal (whole-grain) spelt flour

¾ teaspoon table salt

1¼ teaspoons dried yeast

25 g (1 oz/¼ cup) finely grated parmesan cheese

2 tablespoons finely chopped sun-dried tomatoes

1 egg, lightly beaten

125 ml (4 fl oz/½ cup) milk

60 g (2¼ oz) unsalted butter (preferably grass-fed), diced, at room temperature

To make the dough: Whisk together the flours, salt, yeast and parmesan cheese in a large bowl until well mixed. Stir through the sun-dried tomatoes. Beat the egg into the milk in a separate bowl, then add to the dry ingredients. Bring the dough together using a fork, then add the butter and transfer to an electric standard mixer. Knead with a dough hook for 10–12 minutes until the dough is soft and pliable. Cover with a damp tea towel (dish towel), and leave to rise in a warm place for 2 hours, or until doubled in size.

To make the pesto: Meanwhile, prepare the pesto. Using a blender or food processor, chop the almonds into very small pieces, but not quite enough to be a meal. Add the remaining ingredients, and whiz until you have a thick pesto. Set aside.

To finish the rolls: Line a 12-hole muffin tin with paper cases On a lightly floured work surface, gently press the air out of the

SPINACH AND ALMOND PESTO

55 g (2 oz/⅓ cup) whole natural almonds

100 g (3½ oz/2 cups) English spinach leaves (raw and firmly packed)

25 g (1 oz/¼ cup) finely grated parmesan cheese

juice of 1 lemon (remove pips)

125 ml (4 fl oz/½ cup) extra virgin olive oil

1 garlic clove, peeled

dough, then roll into a rectangle about 30 x 20 cm (12 x 8 inches), with a long edge at the bottom, closest to you. Imagining the dough divided into thirds lengthways, spread about half the pesto down the centre third. Fold in both sides of the dough that have no pesto, one on top of the other, then fold the top and bottom of the dough to meet together in the middle. Roll out the dough so that it is long and thin, with a short edge at the bottom, closest to you. Rolling away from you, roll the dough into a tube. Cut into 12 equal-sized pieces, and place each one in a hole in the muffin tin with the pesto layers facing up. Cover with a clean tea towel (dish towel) and leave for 35 minutes for a second rise.

Preheat the oven to 180°C (350°F). Bake the rolls for 20–30 minutes until they are golden and have popped out the tops of their cases.

For little ones: *Slice these rolls in half for easier gripping.*

PREPARATION TIME 20 minutes, plus 2 hours 35 minutes' rising **COOKING TIME** 30 minutes
⫸ DIETARY INFO Vegetarian

Pork and Potato Hash
with Apple and Cranberry

MAKES 4 ADULT PORTIONS OR 8 BABY PORTIONS

Winter wouldn't be winter without a humble pot of hash on the dinner table. In this recipe I've swapped the traditional corned beef, which is high in salt and preservatives, for some naturally flavourful pork loin and seasonal cranberries, apples, potatoes and herbs.

I've suggested serving this with seasonal vegetables, but truth be told – and perhaps it's my Northern English roots, I'm not sure – I'd usually enjoy this with a chunky heel of buttered sourdough bread to mop up the sauce.

500 g (1 lb 2 oz) all-purpose potatoes, peeled and diced

2 tablespoons olive oil

300 g (10½ oz) pork loin, cut into strips

3 large eating apples, peeled, cored and diced

100 g (3½ oz/1 cup) fresh or frozen cranberries

125 ml (4 fl oz/½ cup) vegetable stock

2 garlic cloves, crushed

1 tablespoon fresh rosemary leaves

1 tablespoon fresh thyme leaves

60 ml (2 fl oz/¼ cup) milk

seasonal vegetables, to serve

Preheat the oven to 200°C (400°F).

Parboil the potatoes in plenty of water for 10 minutes until just starting to soften. Drain and transfer to a ceramic roasting dish.

Meanwhile, heat the olive oil in a large frying pan over medium heat. Add the pork and sauté for 8–10 minutes until browned on all sides. Add this to the potatoes, along with all the remaining ingredients except the milk. Give them a good stir to mix evenly, cover and bake for 30 minutes.

Remove from the oven, mash half the ingredients and stir in the milk to make a thick sauce. Serve with seasonal vegetables.

For little ones: *The pork is cooked for only a relatively short length of time here; if you want it very soft and pull-apart, you'll need to cook it for longer at a lower temperature. Either way, make sure to cut the potatoes and apples into graspable pieces.*

PREPARATION TIME 15 minutes **COOKING TIME** 50 minutes
»» DIETARY INFO Dairy-free option (use plant-based milk) ● gluten-free ● nut-free

Pumpkin and Lentil Patties
with Buckwheat and Quinoa

MAKES ABOUT 10 PATTIES

I believe that to have any real hope of instilling a love of vegetables in our children, they need to regularly see and enjoy them as the heart of the meal, rather than as a side. These patties are entirely plant-powered and prove, I think, that vegan food can be delicious and satisfying. The recipe will reap a good batch of patties that will freeze well.

200 g (7 oz/1 cup) split red lentils

85 g (3 oz/½ cup) raw buckwheat groats (see note on page 105), soaked for at least 1 hour beforehand

2 tablespoons olive oil, plus extra for frying

1 teaspoon ground cumin

½ teaspoon ground coriander

½ teaspoon ground turmeric

½ teaspoon ground cardamom

300 g (10½ oz/2 cups) diced peeled and deseeded pumpkin (winter squash)

1 small onion, finely chopped

100 g (3½ oz) quinoa flakes

2 tablespoons unsalted peanut butter

seasonal salad or vegetables, to serve

Preheat the oven to 200°C (400°F).

Put the lentils and buckwheat groats in a sieve, and rinse until the water runs clear. Pick over the lentils to remove any debris; drain. Transfer to a large saucepan, add 625 ml (21½ fl oz/2½ cups) cold water and bring to the boil. Reduce the heat to low, cover and simmer for 20 minutes until all the liquid has been absorbed.

Meanwhile, mix the olive oil with the spices in a large bowl, and toss the pumpkin and onion to coat. Empty onto a baking tray, and bake for 20 minutes.

Return the cooked pumpkin and onion to the large bowl and add the cooked lentils and buckwheat, quinoa flakes and peanut butter. Leave for about 5 minutes until cool enough to handle, then mash the ingredients and use your hands to form about 10 palm-sized patties. Set aside on a plate ready to fry.

Using a large frying pan over medium heat and allowing roughly 1 teaspoon olive oil per patty, cook the patties for 2–3 minutes on each side until golden brown. You can do more than one at a time to speed things up. Serve with seasonal salad or vegetables.

For little ones: *These are a great first food to try with babies. They hold together well, but are soft to handle in the mouth. They're full of flavour from the spice mix, and the combination of lentils, buckwheat and quinoa makes them very nutritious and filling.*

PREPARATION TIME 15 minutes, plus at least 1 hour's soaking   **COOKING TIME** 30 minutes
⫸ DIETARY INFO Dairy-free ● gluten-free ● vegetarian ● vegan

Creamy Cauliflower Soup
with Parsnip Crisps

MAKES 4–6 ADULT PORTIONS OR 8–12 BABY PORTIONS

A couple of weeks after I had Jonathan, my husband and I took him on a little day trip to the tip of Port Phillip Bay. It was a blustery, grey day and the waves were bashing at the front. We found solace in the shape of a sleepy little French restaurant, where a bowl of creamy cauliflower and celeriac soup, a little like this one, offered much-needed comfort and warmth.

300 g (10½ oz) parsnips

2 tablespoons olive oil

1 onion, finely chopped

2 garlic cloves, crushed

500 g (1 lb 2 oz) cauliflower (about ½ head), roughly chopped

150 g (5½ oz) celeriac (about ½ bulb), roughly chopped

200 g (7 oz/1 cup) cooked cannellini beans, rinsed and drained

1 litre (35 fl oz/4 cups) vegetable stock

125 ml (4 fl oz/½ cup) milk

2 tablespoons extra virgin olive oil

1 bay leaf

150 g (5½ oz) curly kale, large stems removed and roughly chopped

Preheat the oven to 200°C (400°F).

Finely slice the parsnips into coins until they get too narrow, at which point keep the tips whole. Spread out on a baking tray, and roast for 30 minutes, or until the crisps are crisp and the tips soft.

Meanwhile, heat the oil in a large saucepan over medium heat. Add the onion and garlic, and sauté for about 5 minutes until soft. Add the cauliflower and celeriac, and sauté for a further 5 minutes.

Next, add the cannellini beans, stock, milk, extra virgin olive oil and bay leaf. Season with some freshly ground black pepper. Bring to the boil, then reduce the heat to low, cover and simmer for 15 minutes.

Place the kale on top of the soup, replace the lid and steam for 5 minutes, or until the kale has wilted. Remove the pan from the heat and fish out and discard the bay leaf. Carefully use a hand-held blender to create a smooth, thick soup. Ladle into bowls, and top with the parsnip crisps.

For little ones: *The parsnip crisps will be too crunchy for toothless little ones, so serve the soft long parsnip tips instead.*

PREPARATION TIME 15 minutes **COOKING TIME** 30 minutes
≫- DIETARY INFO Dairy-free option (use plant-based milk) ● gluten-free ● nut-free ● vegetarian ● vegan option (use plant-based milk)

Sweet Potato Dal
with Coconut Chapattis

MAKES 4–6 ADULT PORTIONS OR 8–12 BABY PORTIONS

I probably cook dal more than any other dish. It takes little time to pull together, but swapping in seasonal vegetables and adjusting the flavour using different herbs and spices mean that the possibilities are limitless. That said, although we enjoy it year round, there's something terribly comforting about a heaped bowl of nourishing lentils in the midst of a bitterly cold winter.

Prepare your chapattis first, and while the dough is resting get your dal bubbling away on the stove.

CHAPATTIS

200 g (7 oz/1⅓ cup) white spelt flour, plus extra for dusting

30 g (1 oz/¼ cup) coconut flour

1 teaspoon ground cardamom

coconut oil for frying

To make the chapattis: Use your hands to mix together the flours and cardamom in a large bowl, and gradually add 160 ml (5¼ fl oz) water. As you get to the last drops of liquid, add a very small amount at a time to get the right texture – all the flour will have come together and the dough will be slightly tacky. If it feels greasy, you have added too much liquid and will need to add a little more spelt flour to absorb it. Knead the dough for 5 minutes in the bowl or on a clean work surface, then cover with a damp tea towel (dish towel), and leave to rest for at least 10 minutes.

When ready to cook, cut the dough into eight pieces. Roll out each piece into a ball, and dip into a bowl of extra spelt flour. Flour the work surface, and roll out the ball into a thin, almost translucent disc; flour both sides so that you can stack them without sticking, then set aside while you roll the remainder.

Heat 1 teaspoon coconut oil in a large frying pan over medium heat. Place a chapatti in the frying pan. Wait for bubbles to appear after about 1 minute, then use tongs to flip the chapatti over and cook the other side for another minute to ensure that it's cooked through. If you have a gas flame, you can finish off the chapattis

DAL

2 tablespoons coconut oil or ghee, melted

1 onion, finely chopped

2 tablespoons unsweetened desiccated (finely shredded) coconut

1–2 teaspoons ground turmeric

1 teaspoon ground cumin

500 g (1 lb 2 oz) sweet potato, peeled and quartered

200 g (7 oz/1 cup) split red lentils, rinsed, drained and picked over

250 g (9 oz/1¼ cups) cherry tomatoes, halved

1 large handful coriander (cilantro) leaves, finely chopped

by holding them directly in the flame with a pair of tongs for 5–10 seconds. You should notice them puff up. Add more coconut oil to the pan as needed; about 1 teaspoon will do two chapattis.

To make the dal: Heat the coconut oil in a large saucepan over medium heat. Add the onion, and sauté for about 5 minutes until soft. Stir in the desiccated coconut and spices, and cook for a further 2 minutes until aromatic. Pour in 685 ml (23½ fl oz/2¾ cups) water, and add the sweet potato, lentils and cherry tomatoes. Bring to the boil, then reduce the heat and simmer, uncovered, for 15 minutes. Remove from the heat, and carefully mash the sweet potato (or you can keep it chunky if you prefer). Stir in the coriander, and serve with the chapattis.

For little ones: *If your baby is just starting out – and unless you were planning on repainting your walls anyway – I'd recommend going easy on the amount of turmeric you add. You can slice the chapattis into strips and dip them into the dal; mash some dal on top or try rolling a chapatti with some dal inside.*

PREPARATION TIME 25 minutes **COOKING TIME** 15 minutes

⟫ DIETARY INFO Dairy-free ● nut-free ● vegetarian ● vegan

Roasted Pumpkin Pappardelle
with Kale and Cashew Pesto

MAKES 4 ADULT PORTIONS OR 8 BABY PORTIONS

Here, I recommend quickly blanching the kale to take away the bitter edge, before blending it into the pesto. Stirring this through the ribbony pasta and serving with some simple roasted butternut pumpkin makes for a bright meal, perfect in deepest winter.

600 g (1 lb 5 oz/4 cups) peeled, seeded and diced butternut pumpkin (squash)

2 teaspoons sweet paprika

2 tablespoons olive oil

250 g (9 oz) pappardelle pasta

250 g (9 oz) curly kale, leaves stripped and roughly chopped

PESTO

125 ml (4 fl oz/½ cup) extra virgin olive oil

80 g (2¾ oz/½ cup) unsalted raw cashews, preferably soaked for 2 hours beforehand, then rinsed and drained

40 g (1½ oz/¼ cup) sun-dried tomatoes

25 g (1 oz/¼ cup) finely grated parmesan cheese

1 garlic clove

juice of ½ lemon (remove pips)

Preheat the oven to 220°C (425°F).

Combine the pumpkin, paprika and olive oil in a large bowl, and stir through to coat the pumpkin. Empty the pumpkin onto a baking tray, drizzling over any remaining spiced oil from the bowl, and roast for 20 minutes, or until soft.

Meanwhile, cook the pasta according to the packet instructions. At the same time, bring a large pan of water to the boil and stand a colander in the sink ready to collect the kale. While the water is heating, place all of the pesto ingredients in a blender or food processor, and set aside.

Blanch the kale in the boiling water for 30 seconds until it has started to wilt. Transfer to the colander at once, and rinse with cold, running water to stop further cooking, take away the bitter edge and preserve the beautiful colour. Add the kale to the food processor, and pulse for about 15 seconds until you have a thick paste.

Empty the drained cooked pasta onto the baking tray with the squash, and stir through 3–4 tablespoons of the pesto, or more if desired then serve. Any leftover pesto can be kept covered with a thin layer of olive oil in an airtight container. Seal tightly, and keep in the refrigerator for up to 5 days.

For little ones: Pappardelle is a terrific pasta to choose for little ones because its thick ribbons are easy to handle. Depending on the skill level of your learner, you may want to cut the squash into fingers rather than dice for easier gripping.

PREPARATION TIME 15 minutes, plus 2 hours' soaking (optional) **COOKING TIME** 20 minutes
⫸ DIETARY INFO Gluten-free option (use gluten-free pasta) ● vegetarian

Hearty Fish Chowder
with Roast Parsnip

MAKES 6–8 ADULT PORTIONS OR 12–16 BABY PORTIONS

For those frosty days when you want to stay in your pyjamas and curl up in front of a crackling fire, I can't think of anything more comforting than a bowl of this satisfying soup. The potatoes, parsnip and garlic are initially roasted, before joining the fish and stock to make a nourishing broth. The lemony seeds are delicious here. I also like to keep a batch handy to sprinkle on salads or pasta.

CHOWDER

450 g (1 lb) all-purpose potatoes, scrubbed and halved

180 g (6 oz) parsnips, quartered

2 tablespoons unsalted butter (preferably grass-fed), melted

1 whole garlic bulb

2 celery stalks, finely chopped

1 onion, finely chopped

1 litre (35 fl oz/4 cups) vegetable stock

4 sustainably caught skinless, boneless fish fillets (about 500 g/ 1 lb 2 oz) (check for any tiny bones)

½ teaspoon chilli flakes

TOASTED SEED SPRINKLE

55 g (2 oz/⅓ cup) pepitas (pumpkin seeds)

1 tablespoon sesame seeds

1 tablespoon linseeds (flaxseeds)

grated zest and juice of 1 small unwaxed lemon (remove pips)

½ teaspoon dried parsley

pinch of sweet paprika

To make the chowder: Preheat the oven to 220°C (425°F). Line a roasting tin with baking paper.

Put the potatoes and parsnips in a large bowl. Add half the melted butter, and stir to coat. Empty onto the prepared roasting tin, and spread out in a single layer. Slice the top off the garlic and rub this in the butter remaining in the bowl. Place the garlic, cut side up, in the roasting tin. Roast the vegetables for 30 minutes.

Meanwhile, in a large saucepan over medium–low heat, sauté the celery and onion in the remaining butter for 5–10 minutes until softened. Add the stock, fish and chilli flakes, then tip in the roasted ingredients, including the garlic slipped from its skins. Bring to the boil, then reduce the heat to low and simmer for 10 minutes. Remove from the heat, then carefully purée with a hand-held blender until smooth (check once again for any stray little bones in the fish); reheat gently if needed.

To make the sprinkle: Put all the ingredients in a blender or food processor, and whiz to your desired consistency. Transfer to a frying pan over medium heat, and dry-toast for 2–3 minutes, stirring regularly, until the seeds start to crackle. Remove from the heat, and put in a bowl ready for serving. (The sprinkle will keep for up to a week stored in an airtight container.)

For little ones: *Grind the seeds into a fine meal, and stir through the soup. Allow the soup to cool, and serve with bread dippers.*

PREPARATION TIME 15 minutes **COOKING TIME** 50 minutes

⋙ DIETARY INFO Gluten-free ● nut-free

Chicken and Quinoa Bake
with Orange, Carrot and Coconut

MAKES 4 ADULT PORTIONS OR 8 BABY PORTIONS

I've often found that life with young children revolves around nap times. Tired children, like tired adults, aren't much fun to be around, and protecting this sacred rest time supports a calmer day. Meals that I can throw together quickly are essential, so that I can make the most of any auspicious afternoon downtime.

Of course, in my fantasy life this is when I'd sit down with a hot, steamy drink, a spoonful of nut butter and a chapter of a good book. But in reality I'm actually tiptoeing around the house like a ninja, doing the laundry and futilely tidying up toys that will be played with when the children awake.

In deep winter, when the days are short, dark and cold, this vibrant, wholesome bake is full of joy and promises to revitalise. Made with just a handful of understated yet flavoursome ingredients, it comes together in about an hour, needing very little attention.

2 tablespoons olive oil

500 g (1 lb 2 oz) organic free-range chicken tenderloins

1 small red onion, finely chopped

200 g (7 oz) baby (Dutch) carrots, cut into thin matchsticks and parboiled for 10 minutes

150 g (5½ oz/¾ cup) quinoa, well rinsed and drained

3 tomatoes, chopped

400 ml (14 fl oz) coconut milk

375 ml (13 fl oz/1½ cups) orange juice (remove pips)

1 unwaxed orange, unpeeled, halved and thinly sliced (remove pips)

Preheat the oven to 200°C (400°F).

Heat the oil in a large frying pan over medium heat. Add the chicken and onion, and sauté for about 5 minutes until the onion has softened and the chicken is white on all sides. Empty into a ceramic roasting dish along with the remaining ingredients, and stir well to combine the orange juice and coconut milk.

Bake, uncovered, for 45 minutes, or until the quinoa is cooked through and the orange peel has charred.

For little ones: Baking chicken in a stock for at least 30 minutes makes it moist and soft enough for babies to gum and suck, and it has the added benefit of soaking up the flavour of any of the poaching liquid.

PREPARATION TIME 10 minutes **COOKING TIME** 50 minutes

⋙ DIETARY INFO Dairy-free ● gluten-free ● nut-free

Buttermilk Chicken and Kale Pie
with a Pepita-Thyme Crust

MAKES 4–6 ADULT PORTIONS OR 8–12 BABY PORTIONS

This comforting, herby pie is easier than most to make – rather than bothering with kneading, chilling and rolling the pastry crust, you just squidge it into the edge of the tin with your fingers. It doesn't take too long, and I find it strangely therapeutic. Lovely, fat pre-cooked butterbeans could easily used as a vegetarian option instead of the chicken, and other seasonal vegetables instead of or as well as the kale.

PASTRY

260 g (9¼ oz/1¾ cups) wholemeal (whole-grain) spelt flour

155 g (5½ oz/1 cup) pepitas (pumpkin seeds), preferably soaked for 8 hours beforehand, then rinsed and drained

90 g (3¼ oz) chilled unsalted butter (preferably grass-fed), diced

1 teaspoon dried thyme

grated zest of 1 unwaxed lemon

CHICKEN AND KALE FILLING

20 g (¾ oz) unsalted butter (preferably grass-fed)

250 g (9 oz) organic free-range skinless chicken breast fillets, diced

1 leek, finely sliced

2 garlic cloves, crushed

1 tablespoon sage leaves

50 g (1¾ oz) purple kale

3 eggs

310 ml (10¾ fl oz/1¼ cups) buttermilk

35 g (1¼ oz/⅓ cup) grated cheddar cheese

Preheat the oven to 180°C (350°F).

To make the pastry: Put all the pastry ingredients in a food processor. Season with freshly ground black pepper. Whiz for about 30 seconds until combined, then pour in 60 ml (2 fl oz/¼ cup) cold water. Pulse briefly until this is combined. Prepare your pie crust by scooping out a small handful of the crust ingredients and closing your fist to press it into a sausage. Push the crust into the edge of a 26 cm (10½ inch) loose-based tart (flan) tin, and repeat until you've finished the edge. Empty the remaining crust into the bottom of the tin, and flatten this out evenly to form the base. A pastry tamper works well to do this; if you don't have one of those, try a pestle or the back of a spoon. Prick the base with a fork three or four times, and blind-bake for 10 minutes. Do not turn off the oven.

To finish: Meanwhile, melt the butter in a large frying pan over medium heat. Add the chicken, leek, garlic and sage, and sauté for about 8 minutes until the chicken starts to brown and the leek is soft. Remove any tough stems from the kale; discard. Roughly chop the leaves, add to the pan with the chicken and wilt for about 30 seconds. Transfer to the pastry case, and spread out evenly.

Beat together the eggs and buttermilk until smooth, and pour over the pie filling. Sprinkle the cheese over the top, and bake for 30 minutes, or until the filling has set.

For little ones: *The edge of the crust may be a little hard for very beginners, so try offering just the base and the filling.*

PREPARATION TIME 20 minutes, plus 8 hours' soaking (optional) **COOKING TIME** 40 minutes

⋙ DIETARY INFO Nut-free ● vegetarian option (see introduction)

Rosehip Chia Jam
with Cranberries and Orange

MAKES ABOUT 375 ML (13 FL OZ/1½ CUPS)

Unlike a traditional jam preserve, this version doesn't cook the nutritional life out of the fruit, nor does it contain copious amounts of added sugar. Just a little simmer to soften the fruit, chia seeds to help to thicken and set the jam, and a little maple syrup to balance out the tartness of the cranberries and rosehip are all that's needed to whip this up.

I have specified white chia seeds simply because black ones can muddy the beautiful ruby colour, but you can use the latter if that is all you have to hand.

250 g (9 oz) fresh or frozen cranberries

grated zest and juice of 2 large unwaxed oranges (remove pips)

1 teaspoon rosehip granules (optional; see note)

2 teaspoons white chia seeds

maple syrup, to taste

Put the cranberries, orange juice and zest, and rosehip granules (if using) in a saucepan, and stir to mix well. Bring to the boil, then reduce the heat, cover and simmer for 15 minutes.

Transfer to a food processor, add the chia seeds and carefully pulse until the mixture has a smooth consistency. Taste and stir in a little maple syrup to your desired sweetness. Empty into a clean jar with a tight-fitting lid, and allow the jam to cool with the lid off. Once cool, seal tightly and store in the refrigerator. Use within 5 days.

For little ones: *Try a dollop on porridge, spread on bread or serve like a chutney with savoury dishes such as cheese or roasted pork or poultry.*

Note: *Rosehip granules are made from the hips and seeds of roses. Look for them at health food shops, specialist organic grocers and wholefood outlets.*

PREPARATION TIME 10 minutes **COOKING TIME** 15 minutes
⋙ DIETARY INFO Dairy-free ● gluten-free ● nut-free ● vegetarian ● vegan

Roast Beetroot
Hummus

MAKES ABOUT 500 ML (17 FL OZ/2 CUPS)

This sweet, earthy hummus is sure to brighten up many a wrap, and it is incredibly easy to prepare as a big batch. It will keep, well covered, in the refrigerator for up to 5 days.

2 beetroot (beets) (about 350 g/12 oz)

2 garlic cloves, unpeeled

2 tablespoons coconut oil, melted

½ teaspoon sweet paprika

¼ teaspoon sumac (see note on page 161)

250 g (9 oz/1 cup) cooked chickpeas, drained and aquafaba (cooking water; see page 225) reserved

grated zest and juice of 1 unwaxed lemon (remove pips)

65 g (2¼ oz/¼ cup) tahini

80 ml (2½ fl oz/⅓ cup) extra virgin olive oil

Preheat the oven to 220°C (425°F).

Scrub the beetroot and trim off the tops and bottoms, but don't bother peeling. Dice the flesh and empty into a bowl with the garlic (skin on). Add the coconut oil, sweet paprika and sumac, and toss to coat the beetroot. Empty onto a baking tray, and roast for 20 minutes until soft.

Transfer the beetroot and garlic slipped from its skins, along with the chickpeas, lemon zest and juice, tahini and olive oil, to a food processor, and blend until combined. Add the aquafaba a little at a time; use only as much as needed to obtain a smooth consistency.

For little ones: *Perhaps avoid putting them in their Sunday best or a clean white outfit for this one!*

PREPARATION TIME 10 minutes **COOKING TIME** 20 minutes
⋙ DIETARY INFO Dairy-free ● gluten-free ● nut-free ● vegetarian ● vegan

Coconut Crumble Bars
with Poached Pear

MAKES 12 BARS

For me, a crumble is a lazy person's pie – just as delicious but a little less faff. We make them a lot during the cooler months and find them a great way to round off our dinner with a simple, nourishing dessert.

This recipe will make a pile of bars that you can keep in the refrigerator and enjoy as wholesome snacks. Alternatively, simply scoop out the crumble when it's still warm from the oven and serve with plain yoghurt, labneh or perhaps even some creamy mascarpone cheese for a special occasion.

4 pears (about 600 g/1 lb 5 oz)

400 ml (14 fl oz) coconut milk

1 teaspoon ground cardamom

80 g (2¾ oz/½ cup) whole natural almonds

50 g (1¾ oz/⅓ cup) shelled pistachio nut kernels

170 g (6 oz/1¾ cups) rolled (porridge) oats (see note on page 104)

65 g (2¼ oz/½ cup) rye flour or wholemeal (whole-grain) spelt flour

90 g (3¼ oz/1 cup) unsweetened desiccated (finely shredded) coconut

125 ml (4 fl oz/½ cup) coconut oil, melted

10 soft medjool dates, pitted

Preheat the oven to 180°C (350°F). Line a 20 cm (8 inch) square cake tin with baking paper.

Peel, core and roughly chop the pears, then pop in a medium saucepan with the coconut milk and cardamom. Bring to the boil over medium heat, then reduce the heat to low, cover and simmer for 10 minutes until soft. Mash and set aside.

Meanwhile, using a food processor, whiz the almonds and pistachio nut kernels until very finely chopped, then add the oats, flour, coconut, coconut oil and dates. Pulse until the mixture has a crumble texture.

Place most of the crumble mixture in the prepared tin, reserving a handful (about 3 tablespoons) to sprinkle over the top. Press down on the crumble with the back of a spoon to ensure that it's tightly packed. Spoon over the pear filling, and make sure that it covers all of the crumble. Sprinkle over the reserved crumble mixture.

Cover with some extra baking paper to ensure that the top of the crumble doesn't burn. Bake for 15 minutes until cooked through. Set aside to cool, then cut into about 12 pieces. These bars will keep in the refrigerator for up to a week if stored in an airtight container. They also freeze well.

For little ones: *Slice the crumble into fingers for easier gripping.*

PREPARATION TIME 15 minutes **COOKING TIME** 25 minutes
⋙ DIETARY INFO Dairy-free ● vegetarian ● vegan

Baked Apple Doughnuts
with a Tahini Maple Glaze

MAKES 12–16 MINI DOUGHNUTS

I won't fib and say that these doughnuts are anything like the traditional sugary, deep-fried, sticky-finger kind. These are doughnuts in shape alone, but they are full of nourishing ingredients and sweetened with just stewed apple and sultanas. Enjoy these still a little warm from the oven or, to make them especially delicious, try the fudgy tahini-based glaze.

DOUGHNUTS

3 eating apples (about 400 g/14 oz), peeled, cored and diced

85 g (3 oz/½ cup) preservative-free sultanas (golden raisins)

150 g (5 ½ oz/1 cup) unbleached white spelt flour

100 g (3½ oz/⅔ cup) wholemeal (whole-grain) spelt flour

55 g (2 oz/½ cup) hazelnut meal

3 teaspoons carob flour (see page 235)

2 teaspoons aluminium-free baking powder (see page 236)

½ teaspoon unsweetened vanilla bean powder (ground vanilla; see page 237)

1 teaspoon ground cinnamon

145 ml (4¾ fl oz) milk

To make the doughnuts: Preheat the oven to 200°C (400°F). Grease a 12-hole mini doughnut tin.

Put the apples, sultanas and 185 ml (6 fl oz/¾ cup) water in a small saucepan, and stir to ensure that all the fruit is coated in water. Bring to the boil, then reduce the heat to a simmer, cover and cook for 10 minutes. Carefully transfer to a food processor, and set aside.

In a large bowl, whisk together the spelt flours, hazelnut meal, carob flour, baking powder, vanilla and cinnamon until well mixed.

In a separate bowl or jug, beat the milk, butter and eggs until smooth, then add this to the dry ingredients.

Briefly pulse the stewed apples to obtain a pulpy sauce, and add this to the large bowl. Use a metal spoon or spatula to fold all the ingredients together until no flour is visible.

Heap about 2 tablespoons of doughnut mixture into each hole of the doughnut tin, and smooth the tops with the back of a spoon. The centre of the doughnut holes should be showing, and you should aim for your mixture to be level with this. Bake for 20 minutes, or until a skewer inserted into a doughnut comes out clean.

125 g (4½ oz) unsalted butter (preferably grass-fed), melted and cooled

2 eggs

TAHINI MAPLE GLAZE

135 g (4¾ oz/½ cup) tahini

60 ml (2 fl oz/¼ cup) maple syrup

3 teaspoons coconut oil

Leave the doughnuts to cool in the pan for 10–15 minutes, then transfer to a wire rack until ready for eating or adding the glaze. If you find that the doughnuts stick to the pan after cooling, run a teaspoon around each one to loosen. They should then easily drop out with a little shake or tap.

To make the glaze: Fill a small saucepan of water halfway with water and then bring to the boil. Put all the glaze ingredients in a large heatproof bowl (big enough to sit on the pan). Set over the simmering water, don't let the water touch the bottom of the bowl, and stir continuously for about 1 minute until everything is mixed together well. Remove from the heat.

Continue to stir the glaze for a couple of minutes as it cools, then either dip the doughnuts into it or drizzle it over the top. Be careful not to leave the glaze to cool for too long, as it will thicken and be difficult to pour. If this happens, set the glaze over the pan of water again until it softens.

For little ones: *You could not get a more perfect shape for babies to grip than a doughnut.*

PREPARATION TIME 15 minutes **COOKING TIME** 25 minutes

≫ DIETARY INFO Vegetarian

Snacks

A daily rhythm that includes snacks is important
to help tiny tummies thrive. Be it a sampler plate
of hummus, cucumber and pita bread; an omelette
with herbs and a sprinkle of cheese; or easy snack
balls or naturally sweetened muffins, all make the
most of every opportunity to nourish.

Apple, Oat and Linseed Muffins
with Blackberry Swirls

MAKES 12 MUFFINS

This is a nifty recipe that you can easily adapt to use any other fresh or thawed frozen berries to hand. These, along with the grated apple and dates, sweeten the muffins entirely naturally, and with a mix spelt flours, oats and linseeds they are substantial enough to be a wholesome start to the day.

250 ml (9 fl oz/1 cup) milk

10 soft medjool dates, pitted

150 g (5½ oz/1 cup) wholemeal (whole-grain) spelt flour

100 g (3½ oz/⅔ cup) unbleached white spelt flour

75 g (2½ oz/¾ cup) rolled (porridge) oats (see note on page 104

2 tablespoons linseeds (flaxseeds)

1½ teaspoons aluminium-free baking powder (see page 236)

½ teaspoon bicarbonate of soda (baking soda)

2 eggs

125 ml (4 fl oz/½ cup) mild olive oil

2 eating apples, peeled and grated

85 g (3 oz/⅔ cup) fresh or thawed frozen blackberries

coconut milk powder, to dust (optional)

Preheat the oven to 190°C (375°F), and line a 12-hole cupcake tin with paper cases or baking paper.

Gently simmer the milk and dates in a small saucepan over medium–low heat for 10 minutes to soften; keep an eye on it to make sure it doesn't scorch. Use a hand-held blender to purée into a smooth, thick milk base, then transfer to a bowl or jug. Set aside to cool a little.

Whisk together the dry ingredients in a large bowl. Add the eggs and olive oil to the milk base, and beat to combine. Gently fold the wet and dry ingredients together until all the flour has been incorporated. Be careful not to over-mix.

Purée the blackberries with 2 tablespoons water until smooth, and set aside.

Spoon the muffin mixture into the paper cases and fill halfway. Add a teaspoon of blackberry purée to each case, then top with more mixture. Swirl with a fork. Bake for 30 minutes, or until a skewer inserted into the centre of a muffin comes out clean. Dust with coconut milk powder, if you like, before serving.

For little ones: *Quarter for easier gripping.*

PREPARATION TIME 20 minutes **COOKING TIME** 30 minutes
⇒ DIETARY INFO Dairy-free option (use plant-based milk) ● nut-free ● vegetarian

Almond and Apricot Oatmeal Bars
Spiced with Masala Chai

MAKES 12 BARS

Porridge bars seem to be a popular option for baby-led weaning, but having tried a recipe that was essentially a strip of cold, rubbery porridge (not so yum), I wanted to make something appetising that the whole family could enjoy. These are really easy to make and store well – keep a stash for a quick and nourishing snack.

This is another recipe where I've used herbal tea to add flavour – in this case, rooibos chai, which is naturally sweet, low in tannins (nutrient blockers) and caffeine-free. When combined with sweet coconut, dried apricots and sultanas, no added sugar is called for.

1 tablespoon rooibos chai loose tea or 2 teabags

500 ml (17 fl oz/2 cups) boiled water

190 g (6¾ oz/2 cups) rolled (porridge) oats (see note on page 104), plus extra (optional) for topping

120 g (4¼ oz/⅔ cup) preservative-free dried apricots

80 g (2¾ oz/¾ cup) almond meal

45 g (1½ oz/½ cup) unsweetened desiccated (finely shredded) coconut

125 ml (4 fl oz/½ cup) coconut oil, melted and cooled

2 eggs

2 tablespoons linseed (flaxseed) meal

½ teaspoon aluminium-free baking powder (see page 236)

60 g (2¼ oz/⅓ cup) preservative-free sultanas (golden raisins)

Preheat the oven to 190°C (375°F). Line a 20 cm (8 inch) square cake tin with baking paper.

Steep the tea leaves or teabags in the hot water for 5 minutes. Strain or remove the teabags, and carefully transfer the hot liquid to a food processor. Add all the remaining ingredients except the sultanas, and pulse briefly until combined. Stir through the sultanas.

Empty the mixture into the prepared tin, and spread out and flatten the mixture using the back of the spoon. Sprinkle with a few extra rolled oats, if you like.

Bake for 30–35 minutes until slightly golden on top. Allow to cool in the tin for 10 minutes, then remove and slice into 12 fingers. These will keep for 3–4 days in an airtight container in a cool place. Alternatively, freeze the fingers and thaw at room temperature as you need them.

For little ones: *You may want to slice the bars into narrower strips for easier gripping.*

PREPARATION TIME 15 minutes **COOKING TIME** 35 minutes
➤➤ DIETARY INFO Dairy-free ● vegetarian

Oatmeal Snack Balls
with Cranberries and Apple

MAKES ABOUT 12

These perfect little snack bites are packed with wholesome ingredients and take no time at all to pull together. They're great for picnics and popping in your pocket when out exploring.

80 g (2¾ oz/⅓ cup) unsalted raw cashews, preferably soaked for 2 hours beforehand, then rinsed and drained

70 g (2½ oz/⅔ cup) rolled (porridge) oats (see note on page 104

55 g (2 oz/⅓ cup) dried cranberries

50 g (1¾ oz/½ cup) preservative-free dried apple

4 soft medjool dates, pitted

60 ml (2 fl oz/¼ cup) coconut oil, melted and cooled

½ teaspoon ground cinnamon

Put all the ingredients in a food processor, and whiz until the mixture gets clumpy. Empty into a bowl, and shape into golf-sized balls using your hands. Store in an airtight container in a cool place or the refrigerator (although they'll be quite firm if kept this way).

For little ones: *Try shaping into fingers for easier gripping.*

PREPARATION TIME 10 minutes, plus 2 hours' soaking (optional)
≫ DIETARY INFO Dairy-free ● vegetarian ● vegan

Nutty Date Loaf
with Ginger

MAKES 1 LOAF

This simple loaf is crusty on the outside and soft and moist on the inside, and is purposely dotted with plenty of holes that are perfect for catching pockets of topping. The warming ginger, sweet toasted nuts and chewy dates obviate the need for any added sugars. A word of caution, though: blitzing the nuts and then the dates in the food processor can be a very noisy business. Don't do this while any little ones are taking a nap!

120 g (4¼ oz/¾ cup) whole natural almonds

75 g (2½ oz/¾ cup) whole pecans

150 g (5½ oz/1 cup) unbleached white spelt flour

100 g (3½ oz/¾ cup) wholemeal (whole-grain) spelt flour

1 tablespoon ground ginger

1½ teaspoons aluminium-free baking powder (see page 236)

15 soft medjool dates, pitted

4 eggs

160 g (5¾ oz) unsalted butter (preferably grass-fed), melted and cooled

125 ml (4 fl oz/½ cup) milk

Preheat the oven to 170°C (325°F), and grease and flour a 19 x 8 cm (7½ x 3¼ inch) loaf (bar) tin.

Use a food processor to pulse the nuts into a fine meal. Empty into a large bowl, add the remaining dry ingredients and whisk until thoroughly mixed. Set aside.

Blend the dates in a food processor to make a single ball of sticky date paste (you don't need to clean the processor if you have previously used it for the nuts). Set aside.

Using a large bowl and an electric mixer, beat together the eggs, butter and milk until smooth. Add the dry ingredients and the date paste, and continue to beat until everything is incorporated. You'll be left with a thick, sticky batter with small lumps in it (the nut meal and dates, rather than the flour).

Use a spatula to scrape the batter into the prepared loaf tin, spreading out the mixture and smoothing the top. Bake on the bottom shelf of the oven for 1 hour, or until a skewer inserted into the centre comes out clean. Leave in the tin until cool enough to handle, then transfer to a wire rack until cool enough to serve.

For little ones: *Try slicing this into fingers, and top with some creamy vanilla labneh (see page 240), mashed banana or chia jam (see page 199).*

PREPARATION TIME 15 minutes **COOKING TIME** 1 hour
⋙ DIETARY INFO Vegetarian

Seeded Snack Balls
with Carob, Coconut and Vanilla

MAKES ABOUT 12

I love to make a couple of batches of snack balls at the weekend to see us through the week. This recipe is based on seeds rather than nuts, making your pennies stretch further. The carob and vanilla give a slight chocolatey flavour, but there's no caffeine, which is important for little ones.

Toddlers or older children might like to help you by rolling these in the coconut to finish.

105 g (3¾ oz/⅔ cup) sunflower seeds, preferably soaked for 2 hours beforehand, then rinsed and drained

130 g (4½ oz/¾ cup) sultanas (golden raisins)

50 g (1¾ oz/½ cup) rolled (porridge) oats (see note on page 104)

90 g (3¼ oz/1 cup) unsweetened desiccated (finely shredded) coconut

90 g (3¼ oz/⅓ cup) tahini

2 tablespoons carob flour (see page 235)

1 tablespoon chia seeds

1 tablespoon coconut oil, melted and cooled

¼ teaspoon unsweetened vanilla bean powder (ground vanilla; see page 237)

Put the sunflower seeds, sultanas, rolled oats and half the coconut in a food processor. Add the tahini, carob flour, chia seeds, coconut oil and vanilla bean powder, and blend until the mixture gets clumpy.

Empty into a bowl, shape into golf-sized balls and roll each ball in the remaining coconut. Place the balls in an airtight container, and leave in the refrigerator for 1 hour to firm up before eating.

For little ones: *Try shaping into fingers for easier gripping.*

PREPARATION TIME 10 minutes, plus 2 hours' soaking (optional) and 1 hour's chilling
≫ **DIETARY INFO** Dairy-free ● nut-free ● vegetarian ● vegan

Fig and Orange Rolls
with Orange Blossom Water

MAKES ABOUT 20

This recipe makes a big batch of soft, zesty fig rolls that are good to have on hand to satisfy hungry tummies. I have used blackstrap molasses because it makes the rolls a beautiful caramel brown colour, but maple syrup would work to sweeten too – the roll will simply be paler in colour.

155 g (5½ oz/¾ cup) preservative-free dried figs

1½ teaspoons white chia seeds

185 g (6½ oz/1¼ cup) wholemeal (whole-grain) spelt flour

150 g (5½ oz/1 cup) unbleached white spelt flour

grated zest of 1 unwaxed orange

1 teaspoon aluminium-free baking powder (see page 236)

80 ml (2½ fl oz/⅓ cup) milk

90 g (3¼ oz) unsalted butter (preferably grass-fed), melted and cooled

1 egg

1 tablespoon blackstrap molasses or maple syrup

1 tablespoon orange blossom water

Preheat the oven to 180°C (350°F). Line a baking tray with baking paper.

Put the figs, chia seeds and 310 ml (10¾ fl oz/1¼ cups) water in a small saucepan over medium heat, making sure that all the figs are covered. Bring to the boil, then reduce the heat to low and simmer, uncovered, for 10 minutes. Remove from the heat, and use a hand-held blender to purée the figs into a sticky jam. Set aside.

Meanwhile, whisk together the dry ingredients in a large bowl. In a separate bowl, beat together the milk, butter, egg, molasses and orange blossom water. Add to the dry ingredients. Stir with a metal spoon, then bring the dough together into a ball with your hands. Knead on a clean work surface for 3–4 minutes until soft.

Dust a large chopping board with flour, then use a rolling pin to roll out the dough into a large rectangle about 5 mm (¼ inch) thick; cut into horizontal strips measuring about 30 x 9 cm (12 x 3½ inches). With the strips still running horizontal to you, spread the fig jam along the centre of each strip, then layer the top and bottom long edges of the dough over the jam to close. Carefully roll over so that the join is underneath, and press down gently to flatten a little. Use a knife to cut each roll to the desired length – four or five per strip – then spread out on the baking tray, seams on the bottom.

Bake for 15 minutes, then transfer to a wire rack to cool.

For little ones: *Be careful not to overcook, as these will become firm and beginners may find them more difficult to chew. Also allow enough time for them to cool properly – the fig jam can be quite hot.*

PREPARATION TIME 20 minutes **COOKING TIME** 25 minutes
>>> DIETARY INFO Nut-free ● vegetarian

Stocking a *Wholefood Kitchen*

Nourishing foundations are built from a good supply of seasonal fresh foods and wholesome pantry staples.

Whole grains

Poor old grains. They are often perceived as being, at best, nutritionally inferior to other foods and, at worst, some sort of toxic entity our bodies can't deal with. They've had a particularly rough ride in recent times with the rise in popularity of low-carbohydrate, paleo and/or gluten-free diets. Yet grains have nourished and sustained us since ancient times. Evidence suggests that we've eaten them for at least the past 10,000 years or so, and their inclusion in our diets has supported our evolution and survival.

Grains are members of the grass family. Unlike most other plants, which have separate fruits and seeds, in grasses the grain acts as both. As a result, grains house all the nutrients needed to sprout and nurture a plant. When combined with other plant foods, they can provide us with all the essential nutrients that we need to thrive. This is why I consider grains right up there with other wholefood provisions when it comes to stocking a nourishing kitchen.

CHOOSE WHOLE GRAINS

Grains are made up of three main parts: the bran, the germ and the endosperm. Most of the nutrients are concentrated in the bran and germ, with the endosperm, in the centre of the grain, housing

219

mainly starchy carbohydrates to fuel the growth of a new shoot. Milling (refining) grains removes the outer layers of the bran, or the bran and germ, and in so doing discards most of the goodness. It also means that the grain gets digested and absorbed more rapidly, causing an influx of carbohydrates that puts strain on our bodies.

Whole grains retain all parts of the grain and so are more nutritious, slowly digested and more satisfying, but as a trade-off the protective outer layers house oils that can go rancid more quickly. As a consequence, whole-grain flours keep for less time in storage – typically around 6 months in a cool pantry – although they will keep for longer in the refrigerator or freezer.

There are so many different whole grains, all replete with their own catalogue of nutrients, that I can't go through them all here – and it really isn't necessary to do so. Instead, my advice is to include a variety of mostly whole grains in your family's diet, and choose those with the flavour you like. Unless you or a member of your family has a proven sensitivity to gluten (see the 'Food Hypersensitivities' section on pages 52–57), you don't need to worry about whether or not it's in the grain you are eating.

PREPARING WHOLE GRAINS

Whole grains, like legumes, nuts and seeds, contain a number of compounds – including phytic acid, or phytates – that prevent them from sprouting to life in your pantry. This is helpful from a practical perspective, enabling us to store grains for a reasonable period of time, but the downside is that phytic acid blocks the absorption of some minerals such as iron, calcium and zinc.

Traditional societies prepare grains in a way that reduces phytic acid, yielding more nutrients from these foods – skills we need to rekindle if we're to base our diets on a nourishing foundation of plants. The main methods used include soaking in warm, filtered water for 12–24 hours at room temperature, souring (fermenting) and sprouting (germinating), and all in one way or another break down the phytic acid, making the nutrients more accessible.

Note: When soaking most grains, acid can help the phytase enzymes to break down the phytic acid (phytates) more efficiently. This can be achieved by adding a starter culture such as whey (see page 240), or try apple cider vinegar or lemon juice.

Spelt

I prefer to use spelt instead of wheat flour in most of my baking. A distant cousin of common wheat, spelt is an ancient grain that has been used for more than 6000 years. It has a sweeter, nuttier flavour than wheat and contains a broader array of nutrients and more soluble fibre, protein and healthy monounsaturated fats. It's also easier to digest and so is a great choice for little ones.

Spelt is a very hardy grain and naturally resistant to insects, and as a result it is usually grown without the use of harmful pesticides and fertilisers. It's typically more expensive than wheat because demand is lower, the yield is lower and it takes a bit more processing to remove its protective hull.

✕

Rethinking rice cereals

For a long time, iron-fortified rice cereals have been recommended as an ideal first food for babies. I believe that, instead, properly prepared whole-grain cereals can naturally provide more goodness.

First, rice cereal is bland and, as I've hopefully shown, we should be encouraging a flavourful diet in babies – bland food will only foster bland taste preferences. Secondly, rice cereals are also promoted on the basis of being gluten-free. The European Society for Paediatric Gastroenterology, Hepatology and Nutrition, however, advises that

delaying the introduction of gluten has no bearing on whether a baby will go on to develop a gluten hypersensitivity such as coeliac disease, and that gluten can be introduced into the diets of all babies any time between 4 and 12 months of age. Thirdly, the iron in rice cereal is not even absorbed particularly well. Lastly, being a highly processed product, rice cereal has a high GI, so it is digested and absorbed more quickly than the body can deal with efficiently.

The other thing I am concerned about is arsenic. A recent study published in the prestigious *Journal of the American Medical Association* found that babies who frequently ate rice cereal had arsenic levels more than three times higher than those who did not, and levels were twice as high in those who ate rice-based snacks such as rice cakes.

Arsenic is an element that is present in water, air and soil. It exists in two forms: organic and inorganic (this has nothing to do with the presence of pesticides and simply relates to whether it's bound to carbon or not). Inorganic arsenic is more toxic. It's a known carcinogen and government agencies, including the US Food and Drug Administration, have acknowledged that it can have adverse effects on baby and child development and pregnancy outcomes.

Arsenic is found in many foods, but rice typically has levels ten times higher than other foods because of the way it grows in flooded paddies and its efficiency at soaking up arsenic from the water. Note, too, that most of the arsenic gets stored in the bran layer, and so brown rice can have more than twice the amount of arsenic as white rice, where the bran is removed through milling.

So far, no health department seems to be advocating a complete avoidance of rice and rice products in the diets of little ones and during pregnancy, but the UK Department of Health does advise against rice milk until a child is at least 5 years old. Nevertheless, given the mounting evidence, I felt it prudent to leave out rice in any of the recipes in this book, and have provided ideas of fuss-free ways to substitute other grains, such as making risotto using buckwheat (see page 111). The only rice-containing ingredient I've used is white miso, in very small quantities. If you're after a flavourful, naturally nutritious substitute for rice cereal, try the sticky Quinoa and Coconut Porridge (see page 179).

Nuts and seeds

Like grains and legumes, nuts and seeds are packed with the nutrients needed to grow a new plant. Most are rich in protein, along with healthy fats and some vitamins and minerals, including the antioxidant vitamin E, calcium, iron and zinc. Linseeds (flaxseeds), hempseeds, chia seeds, walnuts and their oils are also especially rich in essential omega-3 fats.

The healthy fats in nuts and seeds mean that they're prone to going rancid quite quickly, producing chemicals that pose a health hazard. To avoid this, buy nuts and seeds in small amounts in their whole

Tahini

Made in the same way that you would make nut butter, tahini is simply ground-up sesame seeds, and it's packed with plenty of vitamins and minerals, including calcium and iron. You can purchase tahini unhulled (sometimes called sesame butter) or hulled; the latter is thinner and milder in flavour – start with this if you haven't tried tahini before.

Tahini is incredibly versatile – it can be used in dips such as hummus and to boost soups or sauces. Try it drizzled over your morning grains or spread on toast.

✕

form, and replenish only as needed. Both will keep for around 3 months in a sealed glass jar in the pantry, but you can extend their life in the refrigerator to 6 months and even up to a year if frozen.

I'm always reluctant to buy any nut or seed meal that hasn't been stored in the refrigerator. (All too often have I bought some, only to open a bag at home and realise that the meal is rancid.) All you need to make your own is a food processor; for smaller seeds such as linseeds (flaxseeds), a coffee grinder works better. Making nut and seed meals, butters and pastes at home is also a good idea, instead of buying them ready-made. Make sure that you store any meal, butters or pastes in the refrigerator.

You can also make a nut or seed milk quite easily at home. Combine a ratio of 1 part nuts or seeds to 4 parts water (use slightly less water if you want a creamier result). Blend until smooth, then strain through a clean, undyed baby muslin or cheesecloth if required.

Nuts and seeds, like grains and legumes, contain anti-nutrients such as phytates and lectins. Reduce these as you would with grains by soaking them in filtered water with a little salt or a strip of kombu for a few hours; lightly roasting them can also help. If you see 'activated' nuts or seeds for sale (which always conjures up an image in my mind of them holding little placards and chanting), these have been pre-soaked and dehydrated for your convenience (and expense!).

Whole nuts and large seeds pose a choking risk and should not be offered to babies and young children. Little bitty seeds such as chia, sesame seeds and hempseeds are fine, as are nut meals and finely chopped nuts and seeds.

Legumes – beans, peas, lentils and soya beans

Fresh legumes such as peas, broad beans and edamame, and dried legumes (often referred to as pulses) such as lentils, chickpeas and black beans are all key sources of protein in a plant-based diet. Collectively this group also provides us with an array of micronutrients – for instance, B vitamins and iron, calcium and zinc. It's not uncommon to be a bit 'gassy' after eating some legumes. The root cause of this is a group of starchy carbohydrates (sometimes called prebiotics) that manage to escape digestion and find their way into our large intestine. Here our good bacteria ferment them and produce gases as they do so.

Most people find that, as legumes are eaten more regularly, their body becomes more proficient at dealing with them, and any discomfort reduces. With pulses (except lentils, dried mung beans and split peas), soak in warm, filtered water with a little added salt or a strip of kombu for 8–12 hours, then rinse and drain before cooking until tender.

Alternatively, buy precooked tinned pulses, which won't taste as good as dried, but can be an absolute lifesaver when you're pressed for time, as most of us are! Choose those with no added sugar or salt, rinse and drain well. As with all tinned products, it's advisable to look for brands that flag they have a BPA-free lining.

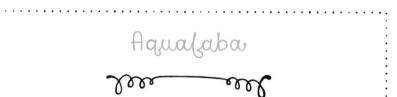

Aquafaba

The word 'aquafaba' comes from the Latin for water (*aqua*) and bean (*faba*). Aquafaba is the cooking water from legumes and is a little bit magic – acting very much like egg whites, it can be used as a direct substitute in recipes such as meringue, mayonnaise, mousses and more to make them vegan. Typically 3 tablespoons aquafaba would be equivalent to an egg, 2 tablespoons to an egg white and 1 tablespoon to an egg yolk. While there are no recipes for these in this book, you'll find that I use aquafaba in my hummus recipes, to achieve a smoother consistency without resorting to water or oil.

×

Tofu

There are four main types of tofu, which differ according to their texture – silken, soft, firm and extra-firm. Tofu is typically made from soya beans (although sometimes chickpeas or lentils are used) and as a result is an excellent plant-based protein source.

All types except silken tofu are made in much the same way that cheese is made from milk curds. Silken is a bit different and is much lighter and sweeter, and more like a thick cream.

Once opened, tofu can be stored, covered with water, in an airtight container for up to a week – you just need to change the water daily.

✕

Fruit and vegetables

Buying organic food whenever possible is important to me, especially when choosing fruit and vegetables because of possible exposure to pesticides. Studies have found that children who eat conventionally produced foods have significantly higher levels of pesticides in their urine than children who eat organic. And although we know very little about how this could impact their health and development, adult farm workers with chronic exposure to pesticides definitely suffer ill effects as a consequence. Thoroughly rinsing conventional produce goes some way towards reducing some of the pesticide residues, and this step should never be skipped, even with organic produce, because of bacteria that may also be present.

Toxic chemicals aside, the main reason for choosing organic is that it's appreciably more environmentally sound – solving rather than creating environmental problems and resulting in a host of wider benefits for earth, water and wildlife.

Biodynamic is one step beyond organic farming, integrating all aspects of environmental stewardship in a holistic approach. It does this in a way that is mindful of nature's rhythms, such as sowing and harvesting according to lunar cycles. Certified biodynamic products will be labelled with the Demeter International trademark.

Dates

An ancient food source in the Middle East, dates have been cultivated for more than 5000 years. You'll find various types available, and so it's useful to know the difference.

There are more than 3000 varieties of the date palm, the fruit of which can broadly be split into three main groups: soft, semi-soft and dry. Soft dates such as medjool are left on the trees to dry in the sun, then rehydrated with steam to plump them back up. Store these in the refrigerator or freezer in a tightly sealed container. Semi-soft dates such as deglet noor and dried dates such as thoory both contain less moisture than soft dates, and so can be kept in your pantry, although they will last longer in your refrigerator or freezer. I tend not to use semi-soft and dried dates too often because I prefer the moist, sweet stickiness of medjools, but they can be cheaper and they keep longer, so are useful to have on hand if you're looking for something to sweeten a dish.

Despite their high sugar content, dates typically have a low GI and are high in fibre. They also contain a small amount of protein (including all essential amino acids), plenty of minerals (especially potassium, but also calcium, iron and magnesium) and an array of B vitamins.

✕

Both organic and biodynamic foods can often cost more than conventional. This is an investment that I'm willing and able to make but, if this is not possible for you, then providing a rounded diet should not be foregone as a consequence – rooting our diets in a variety of colourful fresh produce that is in keeping with the seasons is the essence of the wholefood way.

Meat, poultry and eggs

If we do decide to include animal foods in our diet, at least choosing organically certified meat and poultry offers greater assurances that the animals have been raised compassionately – in an environment that meets their physical and emotional needs. This includes provision for animals to graze on open pastures or, in the case of chickens, space to roam and find the bugs and worms for which they would naturally hunt as omnivores. Organic standards also restrict the use of non-therapeutic antibiotics.

Conversely, some conventional animal husbandry techniques confine animals to small, cramped and utterly miserable enclosures and serve them carefully engineered feed designed to see them grow as quickly as possible. In addition to this, large quantities of antibiotics may be used to improve growth rates in poultry, pigs and feedlot cattle (although this is banned in the EU) and prevent infections that might otherwise occur in such overcrowded and unsanitary living conditions.

Agricultural antibiotic use is contributing greatly to the growing problem of antimicrobial resistance in both animals and humans. This means that in a short space of time our arsenal of effective antibiotics is being depleted, and it won't be long before we're unable to treat what we now perceive as 'small' infections – increasing disease and suffering for both humans and animals.

What's more, in thinking of how important a balanced gut microbiota is to our health, the same can undoubtedly be said for animals. We reap what we sow, as it were. Raising animals in a way that is as close to their natural environment as possible ensures that they are healthier. This is then reflected in the nutritional qualities of their meat, milk and eggs – for instance, greater amounts of essential omega-3 fats.

When it comes to eggs, it's important to cook them through until the white is completely set and the yolk begins to thicken. Babies and young children should also not be given homemade foods that use raw egg as an ingredient, such as mayonnaise or ice cream. This is due to possible contamination with salmonella and a baby's underdeveloped immune system being less equipped to deal with such an infection.

A NOTE ON PROCESSED MEATS

In line with recommendations from the World Cancer Research Fund, processed meat – that is, meat preserved by smoking, curing, salting or the addition of preservatives, such as ham, sausages and bacon – should rarely, if ever, be given to babies or children.

Processed meats are high in salt, which promptly precludes them, but in addition they typically contain nitrates and nitrites. These are converted to carcinogenic nitrosamines, the consumption of which has been strongly linked to an increased risk of colorectal cancer.

Dairy foods

As with meat, poultry and eggs, the nourishment in dairy foods such as milk, yoghurt and cheese is built from the ground up. Organically certified foods will invariably guarantee a higher level of animal welfare, and this will be matched by a superior nutritional profile.

All cheeses have salt added, and so we do need to be mindful of how much we give to little ones. Generally speaking, the harder the cheese and the longer it's been matured, the higher the salt content. That said, these cheeses tend to have a much stronger flavour and so you can use less.

Organically certified foods will invariably guarantee a higher level of animal welfare, and this will be matched with a superior nutritional profile.

Try making labneh, a fresh cheese made from strained yoghurt, at home (see page 240). It has no added salt, is wonderful in place of cream cheese, and you can flavour it with herbs or sweet spices such as cinnamon or vanilla, depending on how you want to use it.

Cultured dairy foods such as buttermilk, yoghurt, kefir and cultured butter have been lightly fermented with lactic acid bacteria, giving them a distinctive tart flavour. If 'live cultures' are stipulated on the label, this indicates that the product may contain beneficial probiotic bacteria. Fermented dairy products are particularly helpful for sufferers of lactose intolerance, as the bacterial cultures can predigest the lactose. Choose unsweetened plain full-fat or Greek-style yoghurt, and add your own fresh fruit, nuts, seeds and spices such as vanilla or cinnamon to add flavour.

Milks

From their first birthday, if you are no longer breastfeeding your baby, they can move straight on to full-cream pasteurised cow's milk or an unsweetened plant-based milk (except rice milk) in place of infant formula. There's no need to use specialised toddler formulas, as a varied and balanced diet should provide ample nutrition.

If you do want to use a plant-based milk in place of cow's milk, it is sensible (at least until there's much less reliance on milk for nutrition) to choose those that are fortified with calcium because plant-based milks naturally contain less calcium than breast milk or cow's milk would offer.

A NOTE ON RAW MILK AND RAW MILK CHEESES

As the safety of raw milk cannot be guaranteed, health departments typically advise that it not be consumed. This is especially important for little ones, who don't have fully developed immune systems capable of dealing with pathogens such as *Salmonella* and *Listeria*. Unfortunately, young fatalities from consuming raw milk are reported. The same advice applies to raw milk cheese for little ones, unless it has been thoroughly cooked through before serving.

Fish and seafood

While fish and seafood are excellent sources of protein and essential omega-3 fats, there simply is not enough fish in the oceans to support the amounts recommended by experts for good health. Moreover, many fish stocks are depleted, and so we need to find a balance to safeguard and allow them to thrive indefinitely and support future generations. The best way to ensure that you're choosing sustainable fish is to look for products with the international Marine Stewardship Council (MSC) blue certification logo.

Another issue to bear in mind is environmental pollutants such as mercury, dioxins and polychlorinated biphenyls (PCBs), which travel up through the food chain from the smaller, plant-eating fish to the larger fish such as shark, king mackerel and tuna that consume them. Infants, children and babies in the womb are particularly at risk of exposure to the negative effects of these chemicals because their brains and nervous systems are still developing, so it's best to choose fish that are less affected.

Examples of fish that generally have lower levels of pollutants, higher levels of omega-3 fats and include MSC-certified species include herring, mackerel, salmon and sardines.

Fats and oils

I wrote earlier about the importance of minimising added fats and ensuring that most of them are of plant origin. The final thing to consider would be what you want the fat or oil to do: add flavour; make something firm (coconut oil and butter work well for this because they are solid at room temperature); add moisture; or cook something in directly.

If the recipe requires no or minimal amounts of heat, including baking up to 180°C (350°F), I always use unrefined oils such as extra virgin cold-pressed, which haven't had most of their natural goodness stripped out through processing. When oil smokes, that means it has started to break down and produce carcinogens that

Coconut oil

Although coconut oil is more than 90 per cent saturated fats, well over half of these are made up of medium-chain fats, which are metabolised in a very different way from the longer chain saturated fats found in animal foods. It's probably therefore quite unfair and more complex than simply lumping coconut oil in with animal-based saturated fats that are linked to heart disease. Ultimately, however, coconut oil is still an added fat, and so we should be mindful of its place within a broader wholefood diet.

×

we don't want to be breathing in, let alone eating. This means that, when heating at medium to high temperatures, organic refined oils are probably better options because they're more stable and have a higher smoke point (if the label doesn't say, you can assume that it's refined). I say 'probably' because very high quality extra virgin olive oil can go to higher temperatures than that without smoking.

Rancid oils also pose a health risk. To maintain optimal nutrition, flavour and safety of your oils, buy in small quantities and in dark bottles to protect them from light. Most are best stored in a cool, dark place such as the refrigerator.

Sweeteners

HONEY

Under no circumstances should honey be given to babies under 1 year old because it may contain spores of the bacterium responsible for very rare but potentially fatal infant botulism. Spores make it to the large intestine, where they can germinate, colonise

and produce the lethal botulinum neurotoxin (BTX). After a year, a baby's gut has a developed its own army of bacteria to act as a defence, and so at this point honey is OK in small amounts. Honey is also fine for breastfeeding mothers, as the spores are too large to travel into breast milk, but it's important to wash hands and surfaces properly to avoid inadvertently passing them on to your baby.

MAPLE SYRUP

Although I rarely use added sugars in my cooking, if I do find I need something extra to enhance flavour, maple syrup is my go-to choice. It's naturally produced from the sap of maple trees in Canada and the north-eastern United States, and it has a wonderful caramel flavour along with its sweetness.

Maple syrup contains small amounts of antioxidant minerals such as manganese and zinc, and is one of the few sweeteners that has a low GI. This means that it's digested and absorbed slowly, avoiding any surges in your body's blood sugar levels that can cause long-term health problems.

Be sure that you're buying the real thing and not 'maple-flavoured syrup', which is a cheaper sweetener and doesn't have the same nutritional properties. Once your maple syrup has been opened, store it in the refrigerator (or even in the freezer for longer periods).

Sundries

CAROB FLOUR (GLUTEN-FREE)

Carob trees are part of the legume (pea) family and are native to the eastern Mediterranean. Otherwise known as the locust bean or St John's bread, carob has been cultivated for thousands of years and was used as a food source in both Ancient Greece and Egypt.

The fruits of the tree are long seed-containing pods, which are dry-roasted and finely milled to make a flour (powder). The seeds are also edible, and are used to make carob/locust bean gum (E410).

You may have come across this on the labels of any number of food products. One of its functions is as a thickener, and it's used in some specialised infant formulas for babies with reflux.

I like to use carob flour in my baking as a substitute for cocoa or cacao, as it adds a similar flavour and colour, but contains none of the stimulants such as caffeine or theobromine found in the latter. Carob flour has a low GI, is high in insoluble fibre and is packed with minerals, including calcium, iron and magnesium, as well as some B vitamins such as riboflavin, B6 and folate.

MESQUITE FLOUR (GLUTEN-FREE)

The woody shrubs and trees of the mesquite genus are able to produce beans even in the driest of climates, and yet it's a largely underutilised food. Once upon a time, long before the arrival of Europeans, indigenous people in what is now the south-western United States and Mexico used mesquite as a staple food, and it was one of the major if not most important food sources of the desert Indian tribes. It is still used today by the Tarahumara people of north-western Mexico, who are famous for their practice of running long distances in mountainous terrain.

Mesquite flour (mesquite powder) is milled from roasted pods and has a malty, sweet yet smoky flavour that can be used in a variety of ways. Its nutritional content can vary considerably from species to species, and even tree to tree, but it has a typically low GI and is rich in soluble fibre, with appreciable amounts of vitamins and minerals.

BAKING POWDER

Most brands of baking powder contain aluminium salts. As aluminium accumulates over time and is known to be neurotoxic, I think it wise to limit our exposure whenever possible and would therefore advocate choosing a baking powder brand that's aluminium-free. Alternatively, make an aluminium-free baking powder at home using 1 part bicarbonate of soda (baking soda) to 2 parts cream of tartar and 2 parts arrowroot powder.

Carob flour has a low GI, is high in insoluble fibre and is packed with minerals, including calcium, iron and magnesium, as well as some B vitamins such as riboflavin, B6 and folate.

VANILLA BEAN POWDER

Unsweetened vanilla bean powder (ground vanilla) is made from ground vanilla beans, and I much prefer using this to using vanilla extract – especially in 'raw' recipes where the alcohol isn't cooked off. Vanilla is fabulous for adding a rich sweetness to recipes, and I regularly use a pinch in lieu of adding sugar.

NUTRITIONAL YEAST

Savoury and slightly nutty in flavour, nutritional yeast can be used as a vegan alternative to cheese. It's the same strain that bakers use for bread, but because this yeast is dead it will be of no use in making your dough rise. It provides all essential amino acids and can sometimes be fortified with vitamin B12, which is helpful for vegans. I find it an excellent choice in place of cheese when I am looking to keep the salt content of a recipe low for little ones.

MISO

There are many different types of miso, all made from combinations of soya beans or chickpeas and other grains (usually rice) that have been fermented. In this book I've favoured the use of white miso, which is milder and sweeter in flavour and, importantly, less salty than darker versions. A tablespoon of white miso is the equivalent of ¼ teaspoon salt (1.5 g). I use it regularly in broths if I have no freshly made stock to hand, and it will keep in a tightly sealed container in the refrigerator for years.

How to Make
Whey, Labneh & Kefir

Fermenting

When we think about our microbiota and its pivotal role in maintaining our health (see pages 12–14), we start to see the importance of cultivating and nurturing these little life forms to ensure balanced gut ecology. One way we can do this is by introducing fermented foods, which are rich in beneficial bacteria.

Although fermenting might sound risky if you haven't tried it before, nature has been used in this way for thousands of years to safely preserve food. What's more, it is also common in traditional cultures to give fermented grains to babies as first foods. Fermenting greatly improves the digestibility of the food, unlocking some nutrients that would otherwise be inaccessible and increasing the level of some nutrients already present.

For this reason, you'll notice that, for many of my morning grain recipes, I recommend soaking and lightly fermenting overnight. While in most cases you may then go on to cook these ingredients and kill the probiotic bacteria, they will still have worked all their magic, making the food more nutritious for your little one.

We usually group ferments into wild or cultured, although there's a lot of overlap when you get into the detail. With wild you're cultivating the bacteria that exist naturally in the food and with cultured you're introducing bacteria (and sometimes yeasts) into the food and going from there. The bacteria feed off the sugars in the food, producing acids, and this in turn brings down the pH, which then overpowers any pathogens that might be lurking.

The ferments I've suggested in this book mainly use either liquid whey or kefir grains as a starter culture, but there are many other options to explore. Whey is the thin liquid that separates from the creamy curds when milk curdles or sours. It is incredibly easy to make at home and will keep safely in the refrigerator for a good couple of months if stored in a clean, airtight container.

Making whey from breast milk

Given breast milk contains more than 700 species of beneficial bacteria, it can make a wonderful starter culture for your ferments. And it's free! Express some breast milk into a clean glass jar or bottle, cover with a tight-fitting lid and leave in the refrigerator for 1–2 days until the milk separates. Scoop off the creamy top layer (stir it into porridge or a pudding, and so on), to get to the bottom layer of yellow liquid, which is the whey. That's it – done! **Note:** As some diseases can be transmitted through breast milk, ferments made using your breast milk should only be given to your children.

Making whey and labneh from yoghurt

Quite a few of my recipes use labneh – a creamy, fresh yoghurt cheese. As it contains no salt, it's perfect for little ones and making it from scratch also yields a generous measure of whey. Take a clean, undyed baby muslin or cheesecloth, and lay it flat on a plate. Scoop out a large tub of full-fat Greek-style yoghurt (ideally organic) into the centre of the cloth, and bring the edges together to make a pouch. Twist the cloth and wrap the 'tail' around the handle of a wooden spoon (or similar), then secure so that the pouch is dangling. Place the spoon over the top of a large jug or bowl, and place in the refrigerator. Strain the yoghurt for at least a day, but you can do it for longer to make a firmer cheese. All the liquid that collects in the bottom of the jug or bowl is the whey – transfer this to a clean container and store, covered with a tight-fitting lid, in the refrigerator.

Making milk kefir

The word *kefir* comes from the Turkish language and loosely translated means 'feel good' – which is so apt because it does have a way of revitalising you. Kefir grains are fascinating little white spongy balls that are a mixture of bacteria and yeasts. You can buy them quite easily online; just be sure to get the correct ones for the recipe you're attempting, either water kefir or milk kefir.

Use about 1 heaped tablespoon kefir grains per litre (35 fl oz/4 cups) milk, and leave it to ferment at room temperature, out of direct sunlight, for around 24 hours; at this point it will have thickened. Note that you need to leave some space at the top of the jar or container you're using because carbon dioxide gas is produced. Also, as kefir contains yeast, a little bit of alcohol will be produced – keep levels right down by making the fermentation time as short as possible and covering the jar only loosely so that air can circulate.

When ready, strain your kefir through a sieve and retrieve the grains either to re-use in another batch immediately or to store them in the refrigerator. The grains do need tending to or they will die, so if you don't plan to use the grains at least weekly, then popping them in the freezer can be your best bet. Also, kefir organisms do prefer the lactose in animal-based milks so, if you do want to make a plant-based kefir (as I have done with coconut milk), try to alternate your batches so that they get a good feed between times.

You can also get whey from milk kefir and use this as a starter culture in the same way you would use whey from breast milk or straining yoghurt and so on. Kefir will naturally separate as it ferments, and so to get to the bottom layer of whey you simply need to scoop out the curds from the top. If your kefir does separate and you don't want it to, just secure the lid and give it all a good shake.

Nutrition Information
& Recipe List

My aim here is to provide further information on the nutritional content of the recipes, but in a way that I hope is meaningful and therefore useful, for those without a nutrition degree. I have also provided a list of vegetarian (V) and vegan (VE) recipes and next to these flagged any recipes that are an especially good source of vitamin B12 (B12), calcium (C), iron (I), protein (P) and zinc (Z) – nutrients that can sometimes be lacking in diets based predominantly, if not entirely, on plants (see pages 49–52 on vegetarianism and veganism). Note that by 'good source' I mean that a single baby-size portion of the recipe meets roughly a quarter of the daily requirement for a 6-month-old to 3-year-old. Finally, to make meal planning less nightmarish for those dealing with food hypersensitivities, I have also provided lists of the recipes that are dairy-, gluten- or nut-free.

IRON-RICH RECIPES

Almond and apricot oatmeal bars (V) 210
Apple, oat and linseed muffins (V) 209
Baked apple doughnuts (V) 204–5
Baked beef meatballs 87
Bean and minted pea fishcakes 83
Beef and black bean tostadas 72–3
Buttermilk chicken and kale pie 196
Cauliflower kitchari (VE) 158
Charred zucchini and peaches with almond quinoa (VE) 108
Chicken and quinoa bake 195
Chunky minestrone with giant croutons (V) 88
Coconut crumble bars (VE) 203
Creamy chia pudding cups with peaches and dried apricots (VE) 105
Fish curry with lemon naan 118–9

Fragrant chicken broth with broccoli and noodles 125
Gingerbread pancakes with fudgy tahini ice cream (V) 172–3
Golden fish fingers 154
Hazelnut and rosemary galette with beetroot and caramelised onion (V) 142
Kale shakshuka (V) 171
Lemon buckwheat risotto (VE) 111
Lemon curd tart (V) 97
Lemony paprika poached chicken with broccoli and pasta 153
Lentil and root vegetable pies (V) 76–7
Mandarin panzanella with root veg and butterbeans (VE) 180
Miso beef, barley and kale stew 149
Nutty date loaf with ginger (V) 214
Oat and olive oil loaf (V) 69

244

VEGETARIAN AND EASILY VEGETARIAN RECIPES

VEGAN AND EASILY VEGAN RECIPES

Note that the nutrition analysis for
these recipes has been completed
using unsweetened, unfortified soy
milk (however, please note that use of
fortified plant-based milks is generally
recommended, especially for vegans).
If fortified plant-based milk is used,
the nutritional content would generally
closely reflect the nutrients highlighted
in the vegetarian list.

Mandarin panzanella with root veg and butterbeans (I, P, Z) 180
Mango and orange popsicles 94
Melon and cucumber gazpacho with coconut milk kefir (I, P) 91
Mulled apple chutney with figs and blackberries 162
Oatmeal snack balls 213
Oat smoothie bowl with warm spiced chamomile (I, P, Z) 138
Orange and tahini baked tofu (C, I, P, Z) 146–7
Pumpkin and lentil patties (I, P, Z) 186
Pumpkin and persimmon soup (I, P, Z) 161
Quinoa and coconut porridge (I, P) 179
Red capsicum pasta bake (I, P, Z) 79
Refried Bean Burritos (I, P, Z) 84–85
Roast beetroot hummus 200
Roast red capsicum and cashew pâté (Z) 126
Rosehip chia jam 199
Seeded snack balls (I, P, Z) 215
Spiced roast carrot and hempseed hummus (P) 127
Sticky date and carob muesli (I, P, Z) 104
Summer vegetable soup (I, P) 113
Sweet potato dal with coconut chapattis (I, P, Z) 188–9
Sweet potato falafel mini mezze bowl (I, P) 150

DAIRY-FREE AND EASILY DAIRY-FREE RECIPES

Almond and apricot oatmeal bars spiced with masala chai 210
Almond buttermilk porridge with cherry compote 63
Apple and date cake 164
Apple, oat and linseed muffins with blackberry swirls 209
Baked beef meatballs with beetroot and quinoa 87
Beef and black bean tostadas 72–3
Blackberry crumble pots 139
Cauliflower kitchari 158
Charred zucchini and peaches with almond quinoa 108
Chicken and quinoa bake 195
Chicken with herby couscous 114
Chunky minestrone with giant croutons 88
Coconut crumble bars 203

Creamy cauliflower soup with parsnip crisps 187
Creamy chia pudding cups with peaches and dried apricots 105
Figgy bircher muesli with hasselback-style apples 176
Fish and spring veg parcels 75
Fish curry with lemon naan 118–9
Fragrant chicken broth with broccoli and noodles 125
Garlicky roast parsnip, pepita and kale dip 163
Gingerbread pancakes with fudgy tahini ice cream 172–3
Golden fish fingers 154
Heirloom tomato frittata 112
Kale shakshuka 171
Lemon and chia pancakes 66–67
Lemon buckwheat risotto 111
Lemon curd tart 97
Lemony paprika poached chicken with broccoli and pasta 153
Lentil and root vegetable pies 76–7
Mandarin panzanella with root veg and butterbeans 180
Mango and orange popsicles 94
Melon and cucumber gazpacho with coconut milk kefir 91
Mulled apple chutney with figs and blackberries 162
Oat and olive oil loaf 69
Oatmeal snack balls 213
Oat smoothie bowl with warm spiced chamomile 138
Orange and tahini baked tofu 146–7
Pork and potato hash 185
Pumpkin and lentil patties 186
Pumpkin and persimmon soup with sumac roasted chickpeas 161
Quinoa and coconut porridge 179
Red capsicum pasta bake 79
Refried bean burritos 84
Roast beetroot hummus 200
Roast red capsicum and cashew pâté 126
Roast veg and chickpea burgers 80
Rosehip chia jam 199
Seeded snack balls 215
Silverbeet chickpea crepes 102
Slow-cooked aromatic lamb and farro with silverbeet 117
Spiced almond fritters 70
Spiced roast carrot and hempseed hummus 127
Sourdough stuffing with pumpkin and sage 145

Sticky date and carob muesli 104
Summer vegetable soup 113
Sweet potato dal with coconut chapattis 188–9
Sweet potato falafel mini mezze bowl 150
Sweet potato hash browns with baked beans 135
Sweet potato skins stuffed with creamy salmon and sprouts 157
Toasted coconut bread 64

GLUTEN-FREE AND EASILY GLUTEN-FREE RECIPES

Baked beef meatballs with beetroot and quinoa 87
Baked vanilla bean labneh 167
Bean and minted pea fishcakes 83
Beef and black bean tostadas 72–3
Cauliflower kitchari 158
Charred zucchini and peaches with almond quinoa 108
Chicken and quinoa bake 195
Chunky minestrone with giant croutons 88
Creamy cauliflower soup with parsnip crisps 187
Creamy chia pudding cups with peaches and dried apricots 105
Fish and spring veg parcels 75
Fragrant chicken broth with broccoli and noodles 125
Garlicky roast parsnip, pepita and kale dip 163
Grilled paneer dip with broad beans and mint 93
Hearty fish chowder 192
Heirloom tomato frittata 112
Kale shakshuka 171
Lemon buckwheat risotto 111
Lemon curd tart 97
Lemony paprika poached chicken with broccoli and pasta 153
Mandarin panzanella with root veg and butterbeans 180
Mango and orange popsicles 94
Melon and cucumber gazpacho with coconut milk kefir 91
Mulled apple chutney with figs and blackberries 162
Orange and tahini baked tofu 146–7
Pea and macadamia nut pesto 92
Pork and potato hash 185
Pumpkin and lentil patties 186

NUT-FREE AND EASILY NUT-FREE RECIPES

Index

Index

Index

Thanks *to* ...

This book wouldn't have been possible without the enduring support of some special people.

To Rob, I know that in writing this book just as Jonathan was born it was very much like jumping from a family of three to a family of five. Despite all the chaos, you were there when I needed more quinoa from the shop at 10 p.m. and you never complained when you ate mung beans for five days in a row. You keep me focused and grounded and your belief in me has never faltered. Please know that I'm grateful every day for what we achieve as a team and couldn't be without you.

To my boys, Laurence and Jonathan, you are the reason I wrote this book. I want you and your generation to grow up with a deep-rooted love and appreciation of real food. One that brings you joy, as well as sustenance, and keeps you and our planet in good health. So go ahead without abandon and enjoy it for all that it is – it will love you back, I can promise you that.

To Becci Vallis and Becky Hodgkins – the pair of you have been there for me every single day and I cannot imagine my life without your constant support, laughter and utter un-wavering belief in me. You both may be on the other side of the world but you are with me, in my heart, always.

To the wonderful team at Murdoch Books, thank you all for all you do, I feel truly blessed to have you look after my third 'baby'. Special mention goes to Diana Hill, in whom I could not have asked for a more fabulous publisher – always calm and incredibly patient. To Katie Bosher and Siobhan O'Connor, I'm deeply grateful for your kind words of support along the way, your attention to detail, for keeping me on track and being all-round fabulous ladies to work with. To Megan Pigott, I cannot thank you enough for being my design doula, taking my baby and nurturing her into life. All the good sleepy vibes go to you and Katie. Lastly to Susanne Geppert for all your wonderful work on the design.

To the talented Ben Dearnley and Vanessa Austin for working utter magic with the food photography and styling, and to Ross Dobson for all your wonderful work on the shoot and being a joy to potter around the kitchen with. Thanks also go to Vanessa Bean for loaning us the most beautiful ceramics for the shoot.

To the littlies on the shoot and their parents for allowing them to feature in this book – Thea and (Super) Ned Pigott, Millie Wilson and Max Faircloth – what stars you are. Thank you for loving real food as much as we do.

To all my recipe testers for their feedback, especially Becky, Dan, Meghan, Hattie and William, Bridget and Brett, Charlie, Neil, Penny and Noah, Vic, Mike and Benji, Jo, Rich, Reuben and Imogen, Hayley, Dan and Harrison, Sally, Andrew, Oscar and Flynn.

To Bryonie Hollaert, Julie Wise and Katie Roberts for their expert feedback on all things nutrition – a credit to our profession. Thank you.

To Vicki Marsdon, I wouldn't be here today if you hadn't taken a punt on me. For your belief in me from the very start, your guidance and continued support – a huge thank you and big hug.

To Diane Jacob, your words of advice and encouragement sailed with me along this journey, long after our trans-Pacific video calls ended. Thank you for making me realise that of all the ideas, this was the book that I needed to write.

To my family and friends, especially my mum and Liz Clarkson. Thank you for being in my life and sharing in all the highs and lows that comes with motherhood and writing-a-book-hood.

Lastly to you, my reader – I cannot thank you enough for choosing this book and for sharing the belief that what we feed our children truly matters. Not just in ensuring that they grow well but most importantly because it is in the day-to-day rituals of sharing food that the memories of our childhood are rooted and memories should be delicious and messy and wonderful, just like they are.

Published in 2017 by Murdoch Books, an imprint of Allen & Unwin

Murdoch Books Australia
83 Alexander Street
Crows Nest NSW 2065
Phone: +61 (0) 2 8425 0100
Fax: +61 (0) 2 9906 2218
murdochbooks.com.au
info@murdochbooks.com.au

Murdoch Books UK
Ormond House
26–27 Boswell Street
London WC1N 3JZ
Phone: +44 (0) 20 8785 5995
murdochbooks.co.uk
info@murdochbooks.co.uk

For Corporate Orders & Custom Publishing, contact our Business Development Team
at salesenquiries@murdochbooks.com.au.

Publisher: Diana Hill
Editorial Manager: Katie Bosher
Cover design and design concept: Megan Pigott
Project Editor: Siobhán O'Connor
Layout: Susanne Geppert
Photographer: Ben Dearnley
Stylist: Vanessa Austin
Home Economist: Ross Dobson
Recipe Development: Vanessa Clarkson
Production Manager: Rachel Walsh

A cataloguing-in-publication entry is available from the catalogue of the National Library of Australia
at nla.gov.au.

ISBN 978 1 74336 809 1 Australia
ISBN 978 1 74336 871 8 UK

A catalogue record for this book is available from the British Library.

Colour reproduction by Splitting Image Colour Studio Pty Ltd, Clayton, Victoria

Printed by C & C Offset Printing Co. Ltd., China

· ·

IMPORTANT: The content presented in this book is meant for inspiration and informational purposes
only. The purchaser of this book understands that the information contained within this book is not
intended to replace medical advice or meant to be relied upon to treat, cure, or prevent any disease,
illness, or medical condition. It is understood that you will seek full medical clearance by a licensed
physician before making any changes mentioned in this book. The author and publisher claim no
responsibility to any person or entity for any liability, loss, or damage caused or alleged to be caused
directly or indirectly as a result of the use, application, or interpretation of the material in this book.

OVEN GUIDE: You may find cooking times vary depending on the oven you are using. For fan-forced
ovens, as a general rule, set the oven temperature to 20°C (70°F) lower than indicated in the recipe.

MEASURES GUIDE: We have used 20 ml (4 teaspoon) tablespoon measures. If you are using a 15 ml
(3 teaspoon) tablespoon add an extra teaspoon of the ingredient for each tablespoon specified.